>what bothers me **most** about Christianity<

>what bothers me most about Christianity<

HONEST REFLECTIONS FROM AN OPEN-MINDED CHRIST FOLLOWER

Our purpose at Howard Books is to:
• *Increase faith* in the hearts of growing Christians
• *Inspire holiness* in the lives of believers
• *Instill hope* in the hearts of struggling people everywhere
Because He's coming again!

HOWARD BOOKS Published by Howard Books, a division of Simon & Schuster, Inc.
1230 Avenue of the Americas, New York, NY 10020
www.howardpublishing.com

The B & B Media Group, Inc.

ISBN-13: 978-1-4165-9255-6

10 9 8 7 6 5 4 3 2 1

Manufactured in the United States of America

For information regarding special discounts for bulk purchases, please contact:
Simon & Schuster Special Sales at 1-866-506-1949 or business@simonandschuster.com.

Edited by Liz Heaney
Cover design by Cherlynne Li
Interior design by Davina Mock-Maniscalco

To my comrade and confidant, Kevin Webb.

There is a friend who sticks closer than a brother.

Proverbs 18:24

>>CONTENTS

	First Thoughts	ix
01	A Hide-and-Seek God: *It bothers me that God is intentionally hiding*	1
02	An Unreasonable Faith: *It bothers me that reason alone doesn't lead to faith*	23
03	An Evil World: *It bothers me that God allows evil in the world*	41
04	A Lone Savior: *It bothers me that Jesus is the only way to a relationship with God*	75
05	The Science-Faith Smackdown: *It bothers me that science and faith sometimes seem incompatible*	97
06	An All-Too-Human Church: *It bothers me that so many Christians give Christianity a bad name*	123

07 An Old Testament "Bully": *It bothers me that God looks like such a bully in the Old Testament* 141

08 A Misuse of Scripture: *It bothers me that believers consistently misuse sacred text* 161

09 A Torturous Hell: *It bothers me that the Christian faith includes a hell* 193

Final Thoughts: *To Believe or Not to Believe* 217

Acknowledgments 221

Endnotes 223

>>FIRST THOUGHTS

Admitting that *anything* about Christianity bothers me will make some think I'm against Christianity. But I'm not. I love Jesus Christ and am decidedly a Christ follower. However, some of the claims of Scripture mess with me—they are disturbing, unsettling, and raw. Truth be told, I find the whole notion of faith disturbing, yet it captures my imagination.

Faith is messy. Part of me wishes it were more black and white. More tidy. Yet, another part loves the mystery of faith, the unknowing of it. It is the unknowing that makes faith, faith, and the mystery of it all ends up making it like an adventure that smacks of romance. So, many of the things that bother me most about faith are also why I love it, which makes faith a love-hate thing for me (or maybe I have a hint of schizophrenia in me!).

I guess the same goes with just about any area of my life—there are things I love and things that bother me about my relationships, my career, my lawn, myself, my *whatever*. I love that I feel empathy for others and genuinely enjoy people, but I find it disturbing that I don't confront issues when I should and regret when I let myself get trampled on (the downside of being an empathetic soul). I love and hate golf. I love hitting that white ball around the big yard they make for such games, but I hate *how* I play—I'm pretty bad.

Those of us who are married love *and* hate marriage. I love being married and sharing my life with my beautiful, caring bride, who actually likes me. Yet, like most men, I hate not being able to stay selfish and self-absorbed. No guy I know naturally loves putting "her needs" above "his needs." Most parents love having kids but hate how much kids cost. We all love and hate our jobs; love and hate our relatives . . . need I go on?

This is the way of life: it is a love-hate adventure. I am thankful we can focus on and live in the love side of life, which requires both grace and discipline. But that does not mean life isn't disturbing at times. It is.

This is true in the arena of faith as well. Those who embrace Christ love Christianity, but some parts of faith still don't sit well. But not everyone is willing to admit this. Some put such thoughts to the backs of their minds and appear to have a pretend, overly simplistic, Pollyannaish position about faith. They claim they never experience tension or doubt—that their faith is always an ecstatic, absolute, unwavering "knowing" that bubbles inside them at all times—always clean; forever effervescent; never encroached upon with doubt. But I don't believe them.

If we aren't honest about the tensions in faith, problems emerge.

If we aren't honest about the tensions in faith, problems emerge. Critical thinkers observe Christians and dismiss the claims of Christ, and some Christ followers end up living more in the land of fake than faith. That's why I want to talk openly about what bothers me most about Christianity.

But don't misunderstand me. Faith has already won the day in my soul. Something deep within me—like the E.T. phone-home beacon—draws me inexorably back to the pursuit of the holy. But still, some areas of faith throw and disturb me. I invite you to explore these with me. Some of the areas we'll cover have me befuddled to this day; others are less problematic for me than they were earlier in my faith journey. It's not that I'm totally resolved on all these matters, but I have drawn some conclusions that seem plausible and make sense to me.

Then there are some things about Christianity where it's not so much the Christian teaching that bothers me as it is the way people of faith have distorted and misused biblical teachings—and this has given Christianity a bad name. And that bothers me.

You and I will probably not agree on all points (I'm not sure I will agree with me when I reread this in a few years!). You might even argue with me out loud as you read and end up hating me a little. But hang in there. This promises to be both a challenge and great fun, and I think you will be the richer for exploring it with me.

Ed Gungor

01

>>A HIDE-AND-SEEK GOD

it bothers me that God is intentionally hiding

I believe in God most of the time. But I have moments when I wonder if I'm wrong; times when I have a taste of doubt in my soul. Faith is a tricky business. Those of us who embrace it live our whole lives for someone we've never seen, and we believe in things we are convinced of but cannot prove (at least empirically).

This could easily be resolved if God were visible. It bothers me that he isn't. I mean, come on, it would be such an easy matter for God to appear as God every once in a while, in ways that are undeniable. It would sure clear up some matters and show folks who's right (I love being right). I especially feel this way when believing in God gets me labeled as a "crazy" by those who claim that faith in God has as much value as belief in the Easter bunny or tooth fairy.

I wish every person could have a peek at God, even if only once before the person dies. I'd even vote yes for people to see God while they are kids and then, when they come of age, to stop seeing him. Then they could wrestle with whether he is real or imaginary. That would be better than his being invisible. But invisible he is, and he's invisible *on purpose.*

Judeo-Christian thought has a rich tradition concerning the "God who hides."[1] God loves to hide; he loves to tuck himself so completely into the backdrop of life and creation that many completely miss his presence. Isaiah comes right out and says it: "Truly you are a God who hides himself."[2] The Bible records that after Jesus' resurrection, he was with two of his disciples who knew him well, yet "they were kept from recognizing him."[3] Jesus' own disciples had no clue they were walking along the road with the resurrected Christ. He was hiding. God also hid from the biblical patriarch Jacob, who exclaimed, "Surely the LORD is in this place, and I was not aware of it."[4] God often told Israel, "I will . . . hide my face."[5] The psalmists repeatedly lamented how God was "hiding" from them.[6]

But it gets worse than God's hiding his presence. When it comes to his message, he cloaks it in obscurity, making it fairly inaccessible. In one of Jesus' prayers he said "I praise you, Father, Lord of heaven and earth, because you have hidden these things from the wise and learned."[7] What's up with that? Even Jesus' disciples didn't get what was going on: "The disciples did not understand any of this. Its meaning was hidden from them, and they did not know what he was talking about."[8] When teaching the crowds, Jesus would say, "If you, even you, had only known . . . but now it is hidden from your eyes."[9] He claimed, "This is why I speak to them in parables: Though seeing, they do not see; though hearing, they do not hear or understand."[10] God often hid the meaning of his message from people.

After Jesus departed and the apostles began to teach about faith, they alluded to this conspiracy of hiddenness. Paul wrote, "We speak of God's secret wisdom, a wisdom that has been hidden."[11] The apostle repeatedly called the gospel a "mystery" that "was kept hidden in God"[12] only to be "revealed" at a special time to a special group of people.[13]

>>WHAT'S THE POINT?

Any thinking person has to ask, Why would God hide? If, as Paul said, God "wants all men to be saved and to come to a knowledge of the truth,"[14] why would God hide from people or make his message obscure? The whole notion seems counterintuitive. But as I've wrestled with this question, here are the best guesses I've encountered as to why God functions this way.

Allowing Faith to Be Faith

Perhaps God hides because he has chosen to establish a relationship with humanity through the pathway of faith. In order for faith to be faith, God must remain invisible and unprovable to the senses. If God could be seen as plainly as the sun or experienced as unquestioningly as gravity, faith would not be required. God's existence would be an undisputed fact.

The pathway of faith insists that relationship with God is a matter of human free will and not forced or involuntary. Faith can only exist in freedom, where we can choose to believe or not to believe. Because God uses faith as the only modality for connection with him, any relational connection between us has to be the result of choice or free will. As I wrote in the Introduction, if we aren't honest about the tensions in faith, problems emerge.

Because God uses faith as the only modality for connection with him, any relational connection between us has to be the result of choice or free will.

Christian theology sees God as almighty, all-knowing, and everywhere present; and yet, he respects the right of those he created to disregard him. He only wants authentic relationship with us, so he honors our right to ignore him. Authentic relationships require choice. Forced friendships or shotgun weddings do not constitute real relationships. But the choice to discount God would be impossible if God were visible. Why? Because God's presence is ubiquitous—he is everywhere interacting with us, in everything from holding creation intact,[15] to choosing when and where we would live,[16] to causing all the good we know,[17] to giving us "life and breath."[18] Only invisibility affords us the choice to ignore God. Because he is invisible, we have the option, via faith, to leap past that invisibility into a relationship with him.

The choice to discount God would be impossible if God were visible.

Maybe this conspiracy of hiddenness is like the hide-and-seek game children play. God hides; those who want to find him, look for him. Scripture tells us well over a hundred times to "seek the LORD"[19] or to "seek his face."[20] Perhaps the call to "seek" God is a call to this hiding game. It seems that God has rigged the game so that the persistent, dedicated seeker always finds him. God promises to those who seek him, "I will be found by you."[21] Jesus adds, "Seek and you will find."[22] The notion that God is playing hide-and-seek with us is fairly scandalous, yet amazingly brilliant. Maybe this is why faith is partially fun. For me, it's both bizarre and fun to have a relationship with a Being I have "found" but can't see.

The Romance of Belief

Another possible justification for why God hides is that faith involves more than the rational mind; it also involves the heart. Whenever you address matters of the heart, you must push past mere intellect. God's hiddenness requires that faith rest on more than intellectual interaction. Trying to connect with someone unseen messes with your reasoning faculties. To pull it off, you have to plunge deeper into your soul and engage the "what if?" and "maybe" pockets of curiosity within the human heart. Only when this curiosity ascends can a heartfelt "seek" dawn, leading to the heart-transforming "find."

This rumors the enterprise of falling in love. Boy notices girl; girl notices boy. Eyes meet. Interest rises. There's often an unspoken hint of excitement. Why? Because there is hiddenness in the mix. The obscure dissimilarities between the sexes elicit curiosity in the person with an open heart, and curiosity is a great motivator for pursuing a relationship. Some won't go there—it's too irrational, potentially painful and disappointing—so they face life alone. To be sure, relationships have an intellectual component, but they are not just intellectual. They also transcend the rational mind. By the time a man and woman decide to enter into something as serious as a marriage vow, they have shot way beyond the function of intellect. Their wills, their emotions, their imaginations, the part of them that trusts—all these aspects of who they are must weigh in. One could say that entering committed love involves the whole person. And when you give yourself totally to another person, risk emerges. You wonder:

Faith involves more than the rational mind; it also involves the heart.

How will it change me? Will I be happy? Will I get hurt? Am I being foolish? Wagonloads of scary questions; lots of hiddenness. But the risk, the irrationality, the uncertainty, the hiddenness make love, love. Same goes for faith.

Something about the love between a man and a woman mirrors the love relationship we are to have with God. Paul claimed that the romantic relationship is "a profound mystery" that speaks of "Christ and the church."[23] Somehow the clues of God's existence catch our eye, and we suspect he may be real and even reaching out to us. We feel a rush of excitement and anticipation. The idea may have some rationality in it, but it is also submerged in hiddenness, uncertainty, and irrationality. We choose either to keep seeking or to drop the issue. That choice is a critical one indeed.

>>IN GOLDILOCKS FASHION

Though God is invisible, he leaves us clues that point to his existence. He drops hints of his activity all around us. But they are only hints. As you study the biblical record, you see that God loves to spill his life into the world through subtle, almost unperceivable ways. Unless you are actively looking for him, you will most probably miss him.

As silly as it sounds, there is a Goldilocks way in which God sneaks around our world. Let me explain. In the children's story Goldilocks and the Three Bears, Mama, Papa, and Baby Bear came home one day only to discover that someone has been eating their porridge, sitting in their chairs, and lying on their beds. It wasn't until the end of the story that they found out it was Goldilocks.

I think God, in Goldilocks fashion, gets involved with our lives before we notice him. As the Creator and Sustainer of all life, he metaphorically messes with our porridge, sits in our chairs, and lies on our beds. Though we can see and feel the results, we don't get to actually see *him* till the end of the story. The essence of faith is the human commitment to seek the clues until they lead us to the Hiding One. We may only find him metaphysically or spiritually, but find him we do indeed. James wrote, "Come near to God and he will come near to you."[24]

>>NOT LEFT TO CHANCE

What's provocative about God's hiddenness is that God doesn't scatter his clues in the world and then leave it to chance as to whether people will notice them. He guarantees we will. Scripture claims God has predisposed everyone to notice the clues, that on some fundamental level, God has made the clues to his existence "plain to [everyone]."[25] On some intrinsic level, God places an internal awareness within every person born into this world that there is something more, something transcendent "out there." God has rigged the human heart to notice clues that cultivate a suspicion that there is something otherly to be sought and experienced. Paul said that even those who have never heard the good news about God have this inner awareness "written on their hearts."[26] In this way God makes true his claim, "I was found by those who did not seek me; I revealed myself to those who did not ask for me."[27]

God doesn't scatter his clues in the world and then leave it to chance as to whether people will notice them.

This primitive knowing, however, doesn't mean we "see" the

Hidden One or that everyone understands God in the way Christ revealed him in the Gospels. In fact, a story in the life of apostle Paul demonstrates how people can manifest an intrinsic knowing of the transcendent but not necessarily get the God story right.

Although Christ had never been preached in Athens, Paul said the Athenians were "very religious."[28] The city was full of idols and idol worship. Their religiosity was evidence that God has conditioned all people to believe in something transcendent, and it was an indicator that God has rigged the human heart for faith (at least the kind of faith that elicits a curiosity for spiritual matters). Paul told the Athenians that God has always been with them; that he had "determined the times set for them and the exact places where they should live."[29] Paul was saying, in essence, that God was present and working in their pagan culture *before* Paul got there with the gospel. But he clarified that this working was incomplete and unclear without the addition of the gospel. He then pointed to an altar, which had been built to an "Unknown God," and he declared, "I'm here to introduce you to this God so you can worship intelligently, know who you're dealing with."[30]

Paul is saying that the gospel message he preached was designed to bring clarity to who God is and to give instruction as to how God wants people to connect with him. But notice what else Paul asserts. He claims that whether or not people understand what is going on, God is always working in their lives—he is working in the life of every person, in every nation, at every moment. Many just don't know it is the God of the Bible who is working. Hence, they co-opt the God activity that touches them into their own manmade religious stories. Paul held that the Athenians' commitment to religious expression (as confused and false as it ended up being) demonstrated that God was working in them, prompting them so that they "would seek him" and "find him" because he was "not far from each one of [them]."[31] Paul claims that all people are wrapped in God's care, that "in him we live and move and have our being."[32] However, he firmly believed that until Christ is preached, people miss the point and head down false religious trails, while God's true nature remains opaque and shadowy to them. It is the Christian gospel that brings the religious impulse to fruition and salvation. The true God is found.

It is the Christian gospel that brings the religious impulse to fruition and salvation.

>>WHERE DOES FAITH COME FROM?

If seeing God is off the table, where exactly does faith come from? Why did humans begin to believe in God in the first place? When secularists enter the discussion about the origins of faith, they suggest that the idea of God is a human construct—we made him up. Atheist Richard Dawkins writes, "The proximate cause of religion might be hyperactivity in a particular node of the brain."[33] Cognitive psychologist Steven Pinker suggests there may be a "God module" in the brain that predisposes us to believe in God.

Admittedly, both men dismiss faith as nothing more than an impulse across a nerve synapse. Okay. What if one day a scientist discovers that such a module exists? Would that prove God isn't real? No, it would not. The discoveries of how the brain functions didn't disprove the scriptural claim that God created humans to reason and think. Wouldn't finding such a module actually *sup-*

port the biblical claim that God put a spiritual interest or bent within every person? It would not disprove the existence of God; it would simply show us how God has "set eternity in the hearts of men"[34] to begin with.

So, what becomes of the thing God set in the human heart—this possible module? That's entirely up to each person. Paul claimed some people respond with interest and openness to that inner awareness and begin a journey of faith and discovery that is lifelong and full of mystery and surprise. He said others suppress that knowledge because they are interested, not in surrendering their lives to a creator, but in keeping themselves the center of their own universe.[35] Paul described this group when he claimed "not everyone has faith."[36]

When Jesus was here, he knew that people reacted differently to the clues God placed in the world about the kingdom of God. He knew that while some would respond by seeking more evidence of that kingdom, others would blow off the idea completely. Of this latter group Jesus quoted a haunting song. He said,

> We played the flute for you,
> and you did not dance;
> we sang a dirge,
> and you did not mourn.[37]

In other words, these folks would not respond to the clues left by heaven. In this same chapter Jesus talked about the cities he visited where he did miracles. He claimed that if the same miracles had been done in some of the ancient cities that were destroyed because of their rebellion, those cities would have responded to the message of God. The point? Some respond well to the way God tries to make himself known; others do not.

>>WHAT'S YOUR TAKE?

You and I have to decide what to do with the evidence we see in the world. Because God is invisible, all we see are hints of his activity. Based on those hints, we choose to believe or not believe. Mathematical genius Blaise Pascal, who lived in the 1600s, wrote, "If [God] had wished to overcome the obstinacy of the most hardened, he could have done so by revealing himself to them so plainly that they could not doubt the truth of his essence. . . . There is enough light for those who desire only to see, and enough darkness for those of a contrary disposition."[38]

Pascal was saying that people either see or don't see God, based on the direction of their hearts. So, if you are open to the idea of God, you will notice evidence that will encourage you to continue investigating the possibility of his existence. On the other hand, if you are of a "contrary disposition," you will only see evidence that satisfies your penchant *not* to believe in God. This means your view of the world—your way of interpreting the world and making sense of all its varied elements—inclines you toward a particular way of interpreting the evidence about God's existence. We all operate from a particular worldview. Let me illustrate.

Your view of the world inclines you toward a particular way of interpreting the evidence about God's existence.

Imagine coming across a man giving an outdoor speech one day in 1863. If you were a Martian, you would probably place little significance on what was going on. You'd likely assume that humans occasionally like to stand on big boxes and make sounds. If you were a child on the scene, you would hope the speech would be brief. After all, adults' words are always Charlie Brownesque, "Mwa, mwa, mwa, mwa, mwa." You wouldn't have gotten much out of it. But let's say you were a historian from the future. Listening to this speech by Abraham Lincoln at Gettysburg, Pennsylvania, would have definitely carried special significance for you.

The God who hides takes the risk of being ignored by a race governed by free will.

Your point of view, what you think is really going on around you, impacts how you interpret events, what you make of life, and ultimately how you respond to it. So, what in the world *is* going on? What's your take? Is there a God? Is he controlling things? Or do things just happen on their own? What is the back story behind the events you see in the world? Your answer often depends on your worldview.

Jesus was praying shortly before his journey to the cross, " 'Father, glorify your name!' Then a voice came from heaven, 'I have glorified it, and will glorify it again.' The crowd that was there and heard it said it had thundered; others said an angel had spoken to him."[39]

The story claims the voice of God shot out of heaven. Some folks took the view that it really was the voice of God; others took the view that the sound was just thunder, a natural phenomenon. Why the disparity? Differing worldviews. Two people can observe the same evidence and walk away with two different accounts of what is taking place. People shoehorn what they see into the theological or philosophical frameworks they have already bought into. We all come to the party with some presuppositions; no one is exempt.

Some worldviews are based in a belief in God; others are not. Buddhism, Taoism, atheism, Marxism, and existentialism are examples of worldviews that are nontheistic. Worldviews can't be proven because they represent big-picture ways of interpreting and engaging with the world. The core beliefs of a worldview lie beyond anything resembling final proof.

Because this is the way things such as faith work, Jesus wondered if he would "find faith on the earth" when he returns.[40] He wasn't being rhetorical. Jesus had no guarantee this world wouldn't go the direction of those in Noah's day where "The Lord saw how great man's wickedness on the earth had become, and that every inclination of the thoughts of his heart was only evil all the time."[41] The God who hides takes the risk of being ignored by a race governed by free will.

>>THE FUNCTION OF OUR PAST

Our capacity to believe in the notion of God is also shaped by our past. We all come from the land of broken toys, and because we do, we have issues with trust. It's not that we don't want to trust, it's that those in whom we have already trusted have wounded us: parents, friends, siblings, leaders, and so on. It only takes one or two disappointments before our "truster" (the thing that enables us to trust) starts to shut down like a laptop cycling into shutdown mode—it's still running, but it's not going to do anything but shut down.

> We all come from the land of broken toys, and because we do, we have issues with trust.

If you have had a horrific past, faith will be more difficult for you. You may not respond to the clues of God's existence. Don't be too hard on yourself about that. I think God understands this. I think he's okay with the doubts that pop up as a result of what we have experienced.

A person who has been sexually or physically abused by a parent is going to find it hard to understand or feel trust or believe in God. It's not that he or she is not open, it's that the concept of God has been polluted. Parents always play a significant role in shaping a child's view of God. (Perhaps this explains the stern warning given by Jesus to parents about how they approach their responsibility as parents—see Mark 9:42.)

History's most famous atheists—John-Paul Sartre, Albert Camus, Sigmund Freud, Bertrand Russell, Friedrich Nietzsche, Madalyn Murray O'Hair, and Karl Marx—all had difficult relationships with their fathers or had fathers who abandoned them or who died when they were very young. Perhaps this is why believing in a heavenly Father never stuck. Faith would have proved very difficult for them. Parents color our view of God.

The good news is that God will help disentangle this and empower a clean, robust faith within a seeking person's soul. But it will not happen apart from a willingness to struggle through the hurt, confusion, and doubt that such hard experiences foster. In the process, people must refuse to let personal feelings and experiences limit their view of God. Only then will they be able to sort through what God reveals about himself in creation, in healthy relationships with others, and, ultimately, through the sacred Scriptures. Not easy stuff.

>>BEING HONEST

God promises that he can be found by anyone, but as we've seen, there are some prerequisites. A significant one is a commitment to stay true to one's inner self—not the mature, self-made, adult self, but the simple, innocent, created-by-God, inner-child self.

Paul claimed that through creation itself "what may be known about God is plain to [everyone], because God has made it plain to them."[42] In order to find the God who hides, we must be honest about the indicators that clearly point to his existence. As children, we had an inner suspicion that there was a God. Every child looks at the wonder of the universe and asks questions like, who made the flowers? or who put the stars in the sky? Children have a remarkable capacity to quickly, innocently, almost imperceptibly, orient themselves toward the rule of God. To the surprise of his disciples, Jesus taught that children are perhaps more capable of receiving and orienting themselves toward the gracious, renewing rule of God than adults are.[43] Jesus said to his disciples, "I tell you the truth, unless you change and become like little children, you will never enter the kingdom of heaven."[44] As children grow and observe creation, they have a natural curiosity about what is transcendent. What one does with that curiosity is what's important.

Paul argued that creation has "God's invisible qualities" on parade in ways that are "clearly seen" and "understood from what has been made, so that men are without excuse."[45] The problem, as Paul saw it, was that "although [people] knew God," as children, "they neither glorified him as God nor gave thanks to him."[46] Somewhere along the way, they lose touch with that inner awareness and wonder about God. Paul claimed people will either stay in tandem with their God-given inner curiosity and continue seeking more evidence about God, or they will ignore it.

So, we interpret the evidence we observe in the world through the direction of our hearts. Jesus revealed the profile of those who are able to "see" the kingdom of God. They are "poor in spirit," "meek," "merciful," "pure in heart," a "peacemaker,"[47] and child-like. Jesus also said, "Blessed are the pure in heart, for they will see God,"[48] which means that those who are not pure—those who are too sophisticated to stop and give thanks to God—do not get to see him.

What is the difference between a heart that has the honesty to see God and one that doesn't? It's the difference between humility and pride. The Bible says it overtly, "God opposes the proud but gives grace to the humble."[49] The heart filled with pride will not find God, but those who are humble in heart will. When people are humble, open, and willing to admit their own poverty of spirit, the scales fall off their eyes and they begin to see God at work in their lives. Those with impure hearts, full of pride and self-adulation, form spiritual cataracts that blur their capacity to see God. There are no miracles, no divine interactions; just "thunder." The position of our hearts has everything to do with whether God ever comes out of hiding for you and me.

The position of our heart has everything to do with whether God ever comes out of hiding for you and me.

>>THE PROBLEM WITH PRIDE

There are some strong, very intelligent voices trying to persuade people to not believe in God or religion of any kind. In a pugilistic yet compellingly lucid fashion, highbrow atheists are raising their voices, claiming that faith subverts science, saps the intellect, and has proven to be harmful to our children and society as a whole. They claim faith is an irrational, pernicious, nonintellectual position that results in ignorance, intolerance, oppression, bigotry, arrogance, child abuse, cruelties to women, war, and the like. When you read the arguments this group lays out and look past their use of inflamed language and antifaith prejudice, you get the sense that they are reacting to all the evil that has been done in the name of God.

I can only imagine that this breaks the heart of God. He loves these folks as much as he loves anyone else. The problem is, God has chosen faith as the road that leads to discovery of him, not human wisdom or intelligence. Faith demands a childlike, heart-based openness to spiritual reality. When a person ignores matters of the heart and chooses to believe what seems reasonable, he or she ends up shunning the spiritual. That person will never find God. Scripture says, "God in his wisdom saw to it that [people] would never know God through human brillance."[50] God's commitment to faith as the pathway to spiritual discovery is clearly seen by his promise: "I will destroy the wisdom of the wise; the intelligence of the intelligent I will frustrate."[51] He commits to this even though it will "shame the strong."[52]

It's not that God hates people who put their intellect first. Not at all. He is the one who gave us our intellectual capacity. It's that living by reason alone is a self-relying, self-sustaining enterprise, and faith is the exact opposite: it refuses to trust self in favor of trusting in God. In a sense, self-reliance is a rebellion against God. This is why those who hold reason sacrosanct end up seeing faith as folly and want nothing to do with God. Later, in our chapter on eternal judgment, we will see how a person's direction of trust is carried with that individual as he or she enters eternity. Self-reliant, proud people will want no more to do with God when they see his face than they do now when they don't. These are the ones John saw calling "to the mountains and the rocks" in the book of Revelation, crying, "Fall on us and hide us from the face of him who sits on the throne!"[53] They don't want anything to do with God.

>>HIDING ON STEROIDS

When the heart is right, the hiding God will be found. God himself oversees this process. Jesus declared, "No one can come to me unless the Father who sent me draws him." He goes on to say that a person can only have faith when he or she is "taught by God." He continues, "Everyone who listens to the Father and learns from him comes to me."[54] God does not force some to believe while making others doubt. The journey of faith is an interplay between God and the open human heart. Each plays a role.

The journey of faith is an interplay between God and the open human heart.

God teaches about himself in bits and pieces. The secret for getting into this God classroom is simply longing for him, remaining interested and open to the possibility that he is there. Jesus says, "Those who hunger and thirst . . . will be filled."[55] As a person hungers and thirsts, God comes out of hiding. God promises, "You will seek me and find me." But he adds the caveat that the seeker will only find him "when you seek me with all your heart."[56]

God is so committed to the conspiracy of hiddenness that he goes into hyperhiding when people demand physical proof before they will believe. Some of the religious leaders of Jesus' day came to him and asked, "Teacher, we want to see a miraculous sign from you." Jesus responded, "A wicked and adulterous generation asks for a miraculous sign! But none will be given it."[57] When Jesus was brought before Herod, Herod "hoped to see [Jesus] perform some miracle."[58] Jesus didn't go there. At the cross folks gathered to see if Jesus would perform a sign that would prove he was who he said he was.[59] Again, no proof was forthcoming.

The problem isn't with the evidence; it's with the orientation of the heart.

In the gospel of Luke, Jesus tells a parable about a rich man who end up in hell and pleads with Abraham on behalf of his five brothers. He asks that someone go back to the earth from the dead in order to "warn them, so that they will not also come to this place of torment." Abraham replies, "They have Moses and the Prophets; let them listen to them." But the rich man is positive that the historical evidence is not proof enough. He knows his brothers will not listen unless they have physical proof, so he says, "No, father Abraham, . . . but if someone from the dead goes to them, they will repent." Then Abraham shuts the discourse down by saying, "If they do not listen to Moses and the Prophets, they will not be convinced even if someone rises from the dead."[60]

This story is enormously significant in helping us understand how faith works. Those who won't follow the evidence in the world that points to God's existence will not believe anything that would serve as miraculous proof. The problem isn't with the evidence; it's with the orientation of the heart.

To make matters worse, if one is reticent about following the clues that point to God's hiddenness, God goes even more covert. Jesus' life showed us this: "Even after Jesus had done all these miraculous signs in their presence, they still would not believe in him." So what takes place? Jesus said that in response to their unbelief, God made it so "they could not believe." Jesus said, " '[God] has blinded their eyes and deadened their hearts, so they can neither see with their eyes, nor understand with their hearts, nor turn—and I would heal them.' "[61]

Let's say I told you I heard a faint scratching in my ceiling and I believed squirrels had invaded my home. Then I asked you to help me catch them. You could either tell me I was crazy and yell that you need proof the squirrels are really there before you help me look for them, or you could shut up and listen to see if you can hear them. As long as you are screaming, one thing is certain: you will not hear any faint scratching. You will be deaf to the evidence that supports my claim.

The screaming mind of reason or the untrusting heart of the broken soul can preclude people from perceiving the evidence of God in our world. They're making too much noise. These people focus so much on the natural world for proof that they are oblivious to the evidence that is not seen with the natural eye. And God honors their right to stay in that state.

I'm not sure I get why this happens, and it is certainly a scary notion, but God either enlightens or blinds people's eyes to his existence in response to the condition of their hearts! If your heart is proud, you will be blinded. If your heart is humble, you will be enlightened. Paul wrote of those who "suppress" what God has made "plain to them." He said these suppressors "neither glorified him as God nor gave thanks to him," and as a result, their "thinking became futile and their foolish hearts were darkened."[62] Paul said because of the direction of their hearts, "God gave them over" to become "fools."[63] In the end, pride destroys a person's capacity for spiritual hunger and perception.

But then it gets even more complicated. Even when a person is open to following the evidence to God, there is a point where the trail stops cold and the next step is uncertain. The early road of clue-based faith ends in a *Thelma & Louise* cliff leaping end—dare we go for it? Each person has to make a decision at that moment: *Do I turn back or take the leap into the complete unknown?* I wish we could follow the hints of God's existence like a yellow brick road of clues all the way to the face of God. Then God's existence would be provable to the rational part of our minds. But it isn't. We can make persuasive arguments for God's existence with a number of factors (for example, the design of creation, the range of human experience, the longing for transcendence in every person, and so on), but these arguments are not proof certain. We cannot prove God exists like we can prove that 2+2=4. At some point, we must embrace a different kind of faith, one based on revelation rather than clue finding. This kind of faith goes way beyond the interplay of observation and investigation. Revelation comes from the world of the supernatural. The good news is that faith based on revelation ends in an amazing encounter with the living God. But this kind of faith demands a significant leap over reason. Let's look at that next.

In the end, pride destroys a person's capacity for spiritual hunger and perception.

(Better buckle up, Harold.)

02

>>AN UNREASONABLE FAITH

it bothers me that reason alone doesn't lead to faith

Some folks think the notion of a superintelligent, Creator God is essentially and irredeemably irrational. Talk of faith within earshot of this group is like waving a red flag to a bull. It causes them to throw normal conventions of respect and kindness to the wind. These folks passionately attack people of faith as mad and deluded. The whole God argument is seen as a "process of non-thinking" and an "evil precisely because it requires no justification, and brooks no argument."[1]

Because they see no proof *for* God's existence, this group believes that science has consistently proven there is no God. They contend that people who believe in God are superstitious, obscurantist, naive, and in denial about the advances of science. At the very least, atheists see faith in God as infantile—a childish notion that should have disappeared as soon as a person was capable of evidence-based thinking.

If we believers in God are to remain honest, we have to face these criticisms. Is the Christian faith irrational and unreasonable? Is this criticism valid? The answer is yes and no. First, let's talk about the no.

>>IS FAITH IRRATIONAL?

Just because something is mysterious and unknown does not mean those who believe it are ignoramuses or intellectual lightweights. Case in point . . .

Though the evidence is scant, most people believe Banksy actually exists. Banksy is the mysterious, internationally renowned graffiti artist who has painted his distinctive satirical graffiti in cities all around the world. But his art is done covertly, without permission—it is essentially vandalism. Banksy's striking and humorous images are identifiable and usually antiwar, anticapitalist, and or antiestablishment in nature. The subjects he uses include policemen, soldiers, children, the elderly, and animals such as monkeys or rats.

Though his identity is not known, some are willing to pay millions for an original Banksy *anything*. The man does not give interviews; no one knows if he is single or married or where he lives. One reporter, who was sworn to secrecy concerning Banksy's identity, says he interviewed him. That reporter contends that even Banksy's parents have no clue about his work as a graffiti artist and think their son is a painter and decorator.

When you see the detail and magnitude of Banksy's work on sides of buildings and in heavily trafficked public areas, you are amazed he has been able to pull off his feats without getting caught. At the London Zoo, he climbed into the penguin enclosure and painted, "We're bored of fish" in seven-foot-high letters. At the Bristol Zoo, he left the message, "I want out. This place is too cold. Keeper smells. Boring, boring, boring" in the elephant enclosure. Past the security cameras and under the noses of museum staff, Banksy has placed subversive artworks in heavily guarded museums, such as the Museum of Modern Art, the Metropolitan Museum of Art, the Brooklyn Museum, the American Museum of Natural History in New York, and London's Tate Britain gallery. Banksy even walked into the Louvre Museum in Paris and hung a picture he had painted that resembled the *Mona Lisa* (but with a yellow smiley face).

Who is this masked man? Banksy appears to be a dark-artist superhero. One lone gallery in London sells Banksy originals. Though Banksy's identity is a mystery, it is completely rational to believe he exists. No one has ever caught him painting in public, but his creations are everywhere. Researchers run into dead ends when trying to hunt Banksy down, but they meet folks who claim to know him. A skeptic could propose that Banksy isn't a real person at all, that he is the fabrication of a team of people working an elaborate, well-orchestrated hoax. Yet most believe Banksy exists.

Just because something is shrouded in mystery doesn't mean it's stupid to believe it. In fact, it's natural and rational to believe something based on a preponderance of evidence. This natural faith is the result of a simple curiosity that examines the evidence and makes hypotheses about possibilities. This is the same sort of faith that makes a scientist explore the mysteries found in the world of nature. Most people have and express this sort of faith when they encounter mysteries.

Just because something is shrouded in mystery doesn't mean it's stupid to believe it.

The order and complexity of the universe reasonably points to a creator or a transcendent being. But since no one caught the Creator in the act of creating, the skeptic can propose the notion that the whole concept of God is a hoax, and that would be fair as far as the rules of skepticism are concerned. Even though some people claim they know God (like those who claim to know Banksy), such claims don't prove he exists. However, to suggest (as writers like Richard Dawkins and Christopher Hitchens do) that openness to the reality of God is evidence that one is deranged, deluded, and deceived is unfair by anyone's rules. Belief in God's existence is not irrational.

Unreasonable faith isn't just the result of human effort; it is the coworking of an open heart and a sprinkling of divine grace.

Let me point out that simple belief in God does not constitute a faith that has strong conviction. It isn't settled. Such belief is restless and longs for more information and validation. This general belief isn't the deep faith that Scripture identifies as being "sure of what we hope for and certain of what we do not see."[2] Belief in the notion of God is only the first step down the trail to having a transformational, personal encounter with God. This type of faith is perfectly reasonable.

However, when it comes to the deeper faith described in Scripture, the critics are right. It isn't rational at all. At some point, faith calls for a leap past logic and reasoning. Many things have been proven through the scientific method, which rigorously studies the evidence and refuses to allow hypotheses to become beliefs until something is unquestionably demonstrated. In contrast, even though there are clues that point to the existence of God, those God clues will never *prove* God's existence. As we suggested in chapter 1, a person investigating a belief in God will bump into one clue after another, until somewhere along the way a choice emerges. This is faith of another ilk. This kind radically leaps over the lack of empirical proof and believes what one cannot possibly prove. This is unreasonable faith, and we should call it that because it violates the rules of reason. Its roots are metaphysical; it is the stuff of the supernatural. Unreasonable faith isn't just the result of human effort; it is the coworking of an open heart and a sprinkling of divine grace.

>>DISTURBING INDEED

This bothers me, as reason is important to me. I hate coming across like an idiot. I work hard to think strategically and reasonably about my positions on everything from politics to family life. Yet, about matters of faith, Jesus said, "O Father, Lord of heaven and earth, thank you for hiding the truth from those who think themselves so wise, and for revealing it to little children."[3] I want to be "wise" but Jesus is suggesting that intellect sometimes gets in the way of faith. That means there will be times when belief is threatened by reason. As a believer, I have a choice to make: Will I believe even when it seems unreasonable?

This question makes me break out in a sweat. Any answer but no seems foolhardy, and yet my answer is yes. I wish God had made the journey of faith *super* reasonable so that all people—smart or not—would end up believing, simply because faith is so incontrovertible. But as much as I would like it that way, that is not the way it is. On the other hand, if the basis of faith were reason, then faith would be something we could come up with on our own; it wouldn't require any outside help from God. But it does.

> There will be times when belief is threatened by reason; as a believer, I have a choice to make.

>>A DIVINE GIFT

Paul wrote, "Not everyone has faith."[4] He wasn't talking about the natural, inquisitive belief in God that blossoms as one examines the evidence and dreams of possibilities, he was referring to the faith that is based on revelation. Paul claimed this faith was "not from yourselves, it is the gift of God."[5] Transforming faith is not humanly engineered; God distributes it as a gift. It is supernatural. In another place Paul penned, "Faith *comes* . . ."[6] It comes from God to us. And yet human choice is still crucial, because we must choose to receive that gift in order for it to be realized.

The Christian message sounds too good to be true, which means any rational soul would need help to believe it—divine help.

God is always trying to communicate with the human race. Scripture claims he does so through creation, human relationships, history, and even various circumstances we experience. Jesus put it this way, "Here I am! I stand at the door and knock. If anyone hears my voice and opens the door, I will come in."[7] God longs to connect with each member of the human race. Why? Because we matter to God. Scripture claims each of us is a dream come true for God.[8] God has had a plan from the beginning of time, and it involves us.

Critics of faith say that the Christian claim of God's offering this kind of attention to each person is nothing more than our own selfish attempt at wanting significance. They accuse Christians of solipsism—extreme human self-centeredness. They claim that we refused to abandon our childish self-absorption, so we made up God: "If Mommy and Daddy won't keep me as the center of their universe, I'll make up a being who will. I'll call it God." I understand how the skeptic could arrive at this. Truth be told, the Christian message sounds too good to be true, which means any rational soul would need help to believe it—divine help.

Faith that transforms our lives requires something more than what is going on between our own ears. It requires the action of Another. The significance of this cannot be overstated.

>>THE UNIQUE CLAIM OF CHRISTIANITY

Christianity is not just a commitment to live a certain lifestyle or to embrace a different set of philosophical ideas or to be indoctrinated into some specific doctrines. These things are certainly parts of Christianity, and they are important. But if that is all Christianity holds, it is just another belief system, like Hinduism, Islam, or any other religion.

The unique claim of Christianity is that it involves incarnation. *Incarnation* literally means "God with us." Theologians refer to this as God's ontological presence, which is a fancy way of saying God is actually present in the life of the Christ follower. Christianity isn't just a religion loaded with beliefs and some commensurate dos and don'ts. It involves the actual presence of the person of God in us.

Faith means God's presence with us *in time.*

God wants a day in-day out relationship with his people. Jesus came to earth to open a way for the union of God's life with ours. Faith means God's presence with us *in time*. Faith brings a new quality of life, a new way of living to bear on life. This life is not added on to what we experience as ordinary life. Faith is not some superunleaded gasoline that we pump into our human tanks so we can function more efficiently. Nor is faith a new layer of existence that covers up the old. Faith results in a free and gratuitous communication of God's life *into* our human experience. God hangs with us. Faith creates new birth and new creation in the context of real time. This is God and humankind uniting—us living together in what becomes sacred space. This is a divine/human interaction, a relationship of cooperation.

When God joins himself to you, the things you do proceed from both God and you.

When God told Moses to lead the Israelites into the wilderness, Moses answered, "If your Presence does not go with us, do not send us up from here."[9] The focus of faith is being with God, not ethics, philosophy, or praxis. The psalmist said, "My whole being follows hard after You and clings closely to You."[10] Faith in God is about *him*—he is actually present in the mix.

This is difficult to explain, so please bear with me.

Only God can unite himself to another on the level of *being*. We can only join ourselves with others through interactions like conversation or by doing some activity together (one sings bass, another tenor, and we join together in song) or by having a meeting of the minds on a particular subject—this is the human sense of joining.

When God joins himself to you, however, the things you do proceed from both God and you (assuming your heart is full of the kind of faith that fights to recognize and submit to his presence). Incarnation is not simply God operating *with* you; it is both of you acting together *as one*; it is fully human and fully divine. The act belongs to you, and it belongs to God. It is God's action and your action at the same time. God and human are united and act together.

For example, you come home from work exhausted. You face your family, and you feel God's nudge within your heart: *Smile and take interest in those persons!* You feel the inclination to smile because God has already infused it into your heart as though it were your own inclination, and you either follow it or sink back into your own tiredness. If you don't engage, the work of God in you is blunted. But if you do engage, your response becomes an expression of faith that is literally human and divine. It is your personal act of self-expression, but you and God are united, expressing the same love in one act of caring. This is the mystery of transforming faith.

This means that union with God is more than practicing a lifestyle. The life of faith is more than committing to a certain philosophy or doctrine. It is a commitment to cultivate awareness of the impulses of God's person within your heart, while becoming less and less resistant to those impulses. It means that when you think of your human self, you associate less and less with the isolated human self and more and more with the self that is joined with God. This is how you can say along with Paul, "I no longer live, but Christ lives in me."[11] It isn't that you lose yourself, but that you discover your true self in Christ. Jesus Christ is no longer the other who speaks to you; his voice becomes your voice as you surrender to him.

Jesus Christ is no longer the other who speaks to you; his voice becomes your voice as you surrender to him.

Confusing? Yeah. Certainly irrational.

But, oh so cool.

Atheists offer the alternative vision (not nearly as cool) that we human beings are members of a purposeless, uncaring, random, cold universe. They believe acceptance of that view is the most mature perspective. They claim that thinking we are on our own in this vast, godless universe causes us to take more responsibility for ourselves, versus being lazy and trusting that a deity will care for us. And they believe their position is completely rational.

However, atheists must consider a nagging concern if they are to remain intellectually honest: what if the Christian message is true? If there is *any* chance the message might be true, isn't it worth investigating?

>>"ARE YOU JESUS?"

Some years ago, I got into a conversation with a physician that went spiritual after he found out I was a minister. "I guess I'm an agnostic," he said. "I don't deny there is a God, but I can't say there is one either."

"Faith is about catching him, not about making him up."

"I totally get that," I replied.

"Really?" he asked, a bit surprised to hear that from a minister.

"Yeah," I continued. "We are talking about believing in someone who is invisible. The idea of faith leaves things in the realm of 'maybe, maybe not.'"

We chatted for a while about belief in general, and then I said, "Here's the cool thing. God is everywhere, working in everyone's life. People just miss him. He's working somewhere in your life too. Faith is about catching him, not about making him up. Jesus said if you look for him, you will find him.

"Let me ask you a question," I continued. "Was there ever a time in your life when you felt a kind of otherly peace surrounding you? Like something was transcendent around you?"

"Yeah. That's why I love hiking in the mountains. I get up there, and I feel a serene presence . . . nature, I guess."

"That's God. I dare you to try something. Next time you are hiking and you feel that serenity, talk to it. Ask it, 'Are you Jesus?' If it's really him, he will talk back—maybe not in words, but in a way that will be undeniable to you."

I gave him my address and told him to contact me if anything ever happened. He looked at me incredulously, shrugged his shoulders, and said, "Sure."

About two months later, I was surprised to get a letter from him. He said he had been out mountain climbing in the Pacific Northwest and came to a particularly beautiful ridge. As the serenity of the scene hit him, our conversation came back to him.

"I did just what you said," he wrote. "I felt a little silly, but I asked, 'Are you Jesus?' After a moment, there was a response. Not words, but somehow I knew it was him. Some kind of joy exploded in me. What do I do now?"

>>WHY THE RELUCTANCE?

I find it interesting that atheists such as Christopher Hitchens, Sam Harris, and Richard Dawkins spend tens of thousands of hours researching and writing four-hundred-page books attacking a being they have never fallen on their faces to seek. If they did, God would come to them. Jesus promised "Seek and you will find."[12] He is throwing down the gauntlet. Anyone can search this out to see if it is true; and if a person does, God will reveal himself. So, why would anyone be reluctant to take up that challenge?

I think the resistance comes from a radicalized commitment to reason. Those who struggle with faith often see reason as the highest human good. I concede that reason is a wonderful gift. Reason separates us from the other primates in the animal kingdom and affords us the wonder of choice. But reason is not our only unique capacity. Humans can also meditate, imagine, be thankful, worship, and the like, all of which affords us the capacity to hypothesize about the eternal. Unreasonable, supernatural faith does not find its footing in reason; its roots are in the aesthetic and imaginative parts of our minds. But those are the parts of the human mind that the antifaith crowd refuses to give way to.

When you approach faith too rationally, you lose something—the mystery, the wonder, the life faith affords.

Those who rely on reason alone miss the wonder and mystery of life. The rational mind is uncomfortable with wonder and mystery. It loves to look at things objectively, in a detached, sanitized way. (Many try to do that with God as well, but it doesn't work—he *designed* it not to work.) Whenever a person locked and loaded with reason encounters something mysterious, instead of enjoying it, he or she will try to analyze it, to figure out the how and why. But dissecting doesn't always yield the best outcome.

I first learned this when I was eleven years old and on a scouting trip. Armed with flashlights, a few of us wandered into the woods after dark to explore.

Joe was the first to spot him. He was a pretty good-sized frog. And he was quick. Flashlights and size 8 feet darted every which way as we scrambled to grab him. Something in us boys wanted to know what was inside that frog, what made that living thing *alive.*

"Don't kill it!" Joe cried. "Take him alive."

I'm sure that frog had no idea he was going to stumble into the midst of a gaggle of earth giants that night, and he did his best to flee, but to no avail. I got my hand around him as he tried to hop between my feet. Then we each whipped out our scout-issued jackknives and begged to be the surgeon.

In a few moments the frog lay dead, his inner secrets lost. To my surprise we didn't gain any greater understanding of Froggie when we opened him up. In fact, we lost something. The interest that had charged the air during the hunt completely disappeared when he lay open and lifeless before us. Objective analysis doesn't always end well; sometimes dissecting just kills.

Faith isn't an abstract absolute; it is a subjective experience with God. It's full of mystery and messy variables. Faith doesn't have to understand in order to enjoy. But that's embarrassing for moderns; we want something more akin to scientific notation or legal code. Yet faith only rings true and makes sense when we are willing to interact with God on a heart level, not just investigate him objectively. When you approach faith too rationally, you lose something—the mystery, the wonder, the life faith affords—not unlike dissecting a frog.

It is the subjective, emotive, messy, mysterious parts of falling in love that capture the human imagination.

Objective understanding and objective truth claims have great value, but so do other kinds of truth claims. Think of falling in love. You don't discover everything that is relevant about love when you try to examine it objectively. There are too many subjective and mysterious aspects to it. And it is the subjective, emotive, messy, mysterious parts of falling in love that capture the human imagination.

Neither can you understand everything about faith when you put it under a microscope of reason. Reason is not the only human good. A relationship with God is more like an amazing love story than it is the discovery of absolute, objective, and propositional truth that can be studied and debated. Faith leads to a face-to-face encounter with God and his love, and when that happens, you end up loving God back. You can't help it any more than you can keep your foot from kicking out when you get thumped on that spot on your knee. It just happens; it's a reflex. John wrote, "We love because he first loved us."[13] Unreasonable faith will cause you to have an authentic revelation of God's love and grace for you, which will mysteriously change you. No one can tell you how. But change you it will.

A relationship with God is more like an amazing love story than it is the discovery of absolute, objective, and propositional truth.

You will never encounter this reality by coldly and objectively theorizing or debating about faith. Faith is too relational. You must interact with it.

But in the modern world, objectivity has become a kind of narcotic to us. We believe the only way to know a thing is through the cool, emotion-free, objective logic demonstrated by *Star Trek*'s Spock. This drives our culture to envision a mechanical, impersonal, purposeless universe that edges out God completely. But isn't there truth beyond objectivity? In many cases, the objective view—which avoids engaging with what one is trying to understand—pales in comparison with the knowledge afforded by a more subjective, interactive view.

Our first family dog, Max, died about ten years ago (I'll spare you the details). You could dig him up and put him under the microscope, and you'd find out a lot about Max from this objective view. You'd discover he was a Border terrier with a grizzle-and-tan coat. You'd be able to tell how old he was when he died, about how much he weighed, and what caused his demise. But there are lots of things you wouldn't be able to tell from your objective investigation. You wouldn't be able to tell how much he loved to play tug-of-war. With resolute determination he'd lock down on one end of the rope, shaking and jerking it back and forth while emitting a continuous, deep, bring-it-on growl. You wouldn't know that Max had no concept of quit. He'd keep that consistent, teasing growl, while shaking his tail in pure pleasure. You wouldn't know all the tricks he knew or how he loved to sing. Microscopes don't tell you such things. They don't catch what can only be known by intersubjectivity or interaction.

Some say we cannot know a thing until we can understand it in rational terms. But some things that lie beyond reason can be known. The apostle Paul wrote, "Now to him who is able to do immeasurably more than all we ask or imagine . . ."[14] There is mystery inherent in faith. The Greek Orthodox Church speaks of *apophatic* theology, a theology that celebrates what we don't know about faith and about God. Paul said it this way: "Oh, the depth of the riches of the wisdom and knowledge of God! How unsearchable his judgments, and his paths beyond tracing out!"[15] Ah, sweet mystery—it may drive the antifaith crowd crazy; it may disturb those of us who prefer objective, rational things; but it still transforms lives.

>>REASON HAS ITS PLACE

All this is not to say that people of faith shouldn't question and seek tenable answers about the things we don't understand. One of the most prevalent criticisms from those who are antifaith has to do with how religious thought tends to breed intellectual indolence—some people get mentally sloppy and stop asking critical questions. While I don't think this is true for the majority, many Christ followers have allowed faith to blunt their curiosity. I think that is both unnecessary and sad.

God gave us brains, presumably so we would use them. Using our brains means we must learn to embrace critical thinking and examination. We are not to accept everything at face value. Instead, we should seek to understand the hows and whys behind what is taking place in the world. We should be honest about the issues related to faith that aren't clear or that we don't understand. We should excel at critical-thinking processes.

>>RECOVERING REASON

Ironically, once you have allowed unreasonable faith to lead you to an encounter with God, faith becomes reasonable again. It makes total sense. Anselm of Canterbury wrote, "For I do not seek to understand so that I may believe; but I believe so that I may understand."[16] He was saying that faith is reasonable, but only after one is willing *first* to bear with some unreasonableness. Modern, rational thought says just the opposite: If you do not understand, you cannot believe; you can only believe what you understand.

I once saw a movie where the characters were trapped on a sinking ship. The only way to safety was to leave the water-free compartment they were in and swim underwater to another area that had an exit. One of the characters in the film had a problem with leaving the cabin to jump into the cold, dark, water-filled belly of the ship. He refused to do so. But the ship was sinking. The other passengers finally convinced him that he must go through water to get to air that would last. For me, this is a good picture of what it means to take the leap into unreasonable faith. It's both scary and unreasonable, like jumping into the cold, dark water in order to save yourself from drowning. But once you do it and emerge on the other side, you are glad you did. And, boy, it sure makes sense then. Faith takes the plunge into unreasonableness before it becomes reasonable again.

Faith is reasonable, but only after one is willing *first* to bear with some unreasonableness.

Happy swimming.

03

>>AN EVIL WORLD

it bothers me that God allows evil in the world

Every one of us encounters pain and suffering. I have lost friends to cancer. I've watched a young mom and dad kiss a precious dying newborn good-bye. I have seen Alzheimer's ravage the mind of a loved one. I've sat in the room where family members wrestled with the gut-wrenching news of a dad's suicide. We all know too many stories of pain.

The past century witnessed the unimaginable cruelty of leaders such as Adolf Hitler, Pol Pot, Joseph Stalin, and Mao Tse-tung, who initiated and sanctioned the brutal torture and murder of tens of millions of innocent people. Here's just one example of cruelty from World War II. An Italian journalist was visiting Ante Pavelić, the pro-Nazi leader of Croatia. Pavelić excitedly showed him a basket full of what looked like oysters. He then boasted it was a gift from his troops—forty pounds of human eyes.[1]

Then there are natural evils—earthquakes, hurricanes, tornadoes, and tsunamis—that kill hundreds of thousands and cause unspeakable pain and suffering. When we hear about or experience such things firsthand, we can't help but wonder: *Where is God? Why didn't he stop it?*

The Christian story claims God exists, that he is all-good, all-powerful, and all-wise. It also holds that God allows pain and evil to exist. This raises all sorts of questions: How can this be? Why is there pain? Where does evil come from? Why doesn't God stop it? Why would God create a world where evil is even a possibility? Is this world really the best of all possible worlds God could have created? If God didn't create evil, why is it here, and why is it so pervasive in the world? If God can do anything, why doesn't he just rid the world of evil? The Gospels record how Jesus healed the sick and the blind—a great start. Buy why didn't he just seal the deal for humanity and destroy sickness and blindness altogether?

What makes matters worse is that the most innocent among us are often cruelly brutalized by evil and suffering. Agnostic-turned-Christian Sheldon Vanauken wrote, "If only villains got broken backs or cancers, if only cheaters and crooks got Parkinson's disease, we should see a sort of celestial justice in the universe (but in that case, of course, no one would care to risk being a villain or a crook). But, as it is, a sweet-tempered child lies dying of a brain tumor, a happy young wife sees her husband and child killed before her eyes by a drunken driver; and in our empathy with the dying boy or the bereft wife and mother, we soundlessly scream at the stars, 'Why, Why?' A mention of God—of God's will—doesn't help a bit. How could a good God, a loving God, do that? How could he even let it happen? And no answer comes from the indifferent stars."[2]

The presence of evil is the strongest argument reason poses against faith. Pollster George Barna claims it is the biggest obstacle for spiritual seekers. The Barna organization once asked a scientifically selected cross section of adults: "If you could ask God only one question and you knew he would give you an answer, what would you ask?" The top response was: "Why is there pain and suffering in the world?"[3]

Some have called the presence of evil the rock of atheism. In his book on suffering and evil, D. A. Carson speaks of those who struggle asking, "If God is both omnipotent and perfectly good, how can he permit such evil? If he is willing but not able to check the suffering, then he is not omnipotent; if he is able but unwilling, he is not perfectly good. The implication is that the very existence of evil calls into question the existence of God."[4]

If God exists and he is good, it doesn't make sense that he would allow evil and suffering. How could God be good and powerful and not stop atrocities such as the Holocaust?

In response to evil, it is quite natural to pray, to call out to God for help. Yet many have found prayer doesn't always change things. Some say unanswered prayer is the result of too little faith. But is that really true?

>>WHEN PRAYER DOESN'T WORK

A lot of Christ followers believe that everything that happens to them or doesn't happen to them is directly connected to how they pray. A few biblical texts seem to support this idea. Jesus taught his disciples to pray to the Father, "Thy kingdom come, Thy will be done in earth, as *it is* in heaven."[5] Jesus is urging us to pray that heaven spills into earth. Heaven is certainly beyond the reach of evil. In that same prayer, he also says we should ask God to "deliver us from evil,"[6] implying that there is a way for evil to be halted in the life of a person of faith. We're told that faith "is the victory that has overcome the world"[7] and that "God keeps [the person of faith] safe, and the evil one cannot harm him."[8] These claims certainly seem to say that if one has enough faith, one can avoid experiencing evil in this world.

If things are going well in your life, this view is encouraging. But what if things start going badly? The idea that your faith is *totally* responsible for how much good or evil you experience can be a heavy weight when your doctor diagnoses you with cancer or when you lose your job or when your marriage falls off a cliff.

The idea that your faith is *totally* responsible for how much good or evil you experience can be a heavy weight.

Then there are the judgments. If you accept that prayer is what controls the world, you will end up believing that every person who has a hard life just doesn't have enough faith. If you can look at a person's pain and assign blame to him or her, you will be hopeful (false as that hope may be) that nothing bad like *that* will ever happen to you because you have faith. But self-protecting judgments and catchall faith promises don't hold up when we face Bible stories like Job's. God said Job was "blameless and upright,"[9] and yet he was mugged by all kinds of horrible circumstances. Job's friends thought they understood why he was in torment and harped on him long about it. Though Job contended that he was not aware of any sin he had done to warrant his trouble, his friends repeatedly asserted that God only "repays a man for what he has done; he brings upon him what his conduct deserves."[10] Job was confused, because he had done all he knew to do in the cause-and-effect world, but he still came up wanting. He had questions. Job's friends couldn't grasp complexity or paradox. They assumed Job wasn't owning up to some sin. But they were flat wrong. The truth is, sometimes faith does preempt evil things, but other times it doesn't. Instead, our faith helps us go through the things we cannot stop.

When I was younger, I used to believe that if a person had enough faith in God, he or she could stop evil. I was a cocky, know-it-all, "victory" preacher; and I had faith down to a science. If you prayed the right way, if you believed the right way, if you came to the right church (the one *I* pastored), you were sure to live a life untouched by evil. And if evil showed up, you just needed to pray harder and immerse yourself more deeply in Bible study. I was young and short on life experience, and it was easy to be dogmatically idealistic. But because as a pastor I was deeply involved with hundreds of lives, it didn't take long for me to discover that faith and prayer didn't always work the way I thought they were supposed to. Faith was not an exact science.

I saw that evil appeared in places it shouldn't and for reasons that could not be discerned. My simple faith schema did not produce the control I thought it should, and I was often left befuddled. Evil is shockingly brutal; on a number of occasions, the horror and unfairness of it took my breath away and sent me spiraling into seasons of numbing confusion and doubt. *Why God? How could this happen?*

It seems that faith doesn't come with cute little red bows that tidy up the loose ends of life.

Yes, I've seen prayer change things, but I've also seen situations where prayer seemed to accomplish nothing at all. Over the years, these experiences have goaded me to redefine, modify, amplify, and even dump a number of the beliefs I thought were forever settled in my thinking. The good news is that I've gotten a little kinder, a little less dogmatic, and a lot more compassionate and patient. But, most important of all, I have become aware that I am not omniscient, and I have gotten more comfortable with the idea that I will never grasp how all this works. It seems that faith doesn't come with cute little red bows that tidy up the loose ends of life.

Because evil is a notoriously tricky concept, I have held off making easy, off-the-cuff judgments about it.

That being said, I still have a voracious curiosity about evil. Why is it here? Can anything be done to push it back? Why is it so ubiquitous? And though I don't believe that a satisfactory answer can be found this side of eternity, I do think there are some thoughts that bring clarity and foster the hope "that in all things God works for the good of those who love him."[11]

>>NOT BLACK AND WHITE SIMPLE

Because evil is a notoriously tricky concept, full of multilayered complexity, I have held off making easy, off-the-cuff judgments about it.

Sometimes we humans are not open to rethinking or recalibrating our views of the world. We prefer black-and-white simple analyses that underscore feelings and biases we already hold as true. We presume there is only one way to look at the world—the way we (or our tribe/denomination) look at it. Hence we dole out oversimplified, fossilized, hackneyed conclusions about why bad things happen in this world. The atheist says, "There is no god," while the theist contends, "It was God's will, and God works in mysterious ways." But trying to wrap up why things are the way they are and why they happen the way they happen with platitudes and fancy philosophical bows (religious or not) just doesn't cut it in the face of merciless evil. Trying to get a grip on the why of pain and evil is anything but black-and-white simple. It's full of colorful nuances.

Remember the 1998 movie *Pleasantville*? In the universe of Pleasantville (filmed in black-and-white instead of color) life was . . . pleasant. Nothing akin to the horrors of war, famine, or AIDS existed there. The bathrooms didn't even have toilets—that would have been impolite. The high-school basketball team never missed a shot, firemen only rescued cats stuck in trees (there were no house fires), families were perfect, and teen sweethearts never went past "first base." Everything, absolutely everything, was perfect in that idyllic little town.

That's the danger with color—it comes with the potential of good and evil.

In Pleasantville everything was simple and clear. Black-and-white ruled. But as the citizens of the town began to explore the joys and sorrows of life, things started turning from black-and-white to color—first a flower, then the surroundings, then people. But with the appearance of color came the dark side of human nature. That's the danger with color—it comes with the potential of good and evil. In response, some folks were willing to do whatever it took to maintain the status quo, to maintain their simple black-and-white world. Their fear and paranoia led to intolerance, hate crimes, and violence against anything colored.

Thinking, cognizing, conceptualizing, perceiving, understanding, comprehending, and *cogitating*—all are words for actions of the mind that are much more complex than indoctrinating. But many people, including atheists and Christians, love indoctrinating. They command people to believe and act in certain ways. These folks are not open to integrating what they believe with what they see or to having open discussions about how truth fits or doesn't fit. Neither are they willing to admit when a belief needs to be examined and changed, or dropped altogether. Such openness is way too dangerous, too colorful. Many just won't go there. But if we are to make sense of the evil we experience in our world, we must.

I think we Christ followers need to do some rethinking, particularly in their views regarding where evil comes from and their understanding of sovereignty, predestination, human responsibility, and how faith influences what God does in the world. Christians need to look at our religious propositions with fresh eyes, beginning with the view that pain is a good thing.

>>THE "NO PAIN, NO GAIN" VIEW

It's simplistic to say that all pain is evil, and yet we often feel that way. However, bad things sometimes look evil at the onset but end up being the back side of a good. Doctors, dentists, teachers, athletic trainers, boot-camp sergeants all know there are times when it is good *not* to be kind. Parents engage in activities that could be perceived as evil, at least by children. We may see our son struggling to tie a shoe, and instead of ending his struggle by tying it for him, we let him struggle until he excitedly declares, "Look, Mommy! I did it!" In this scenario, pain is good.

Bad things sometimes end up being the back side of a good.

One night I came home late from work and my oldest son, Michael, who was about four years old, had already gone to bed. I went up to his room to give him a goodnight kiss, but he was already asleep. As I leaned over to kiss him on his forehead, I smelled a minty-fresh odor. I knew that smell. Michael loved a particular mint chewy candy that I often bought for him. He'd apparently grabbed a handful of those minty delights before jumping into bed. As I pulled his lips apart, I saw his teeth were all gooed up with the gumlike candy. I had an instant vision of my son sitting in the dentist chair, crying as the drill whirled. I woke him up and made him go to the bathroom to brush his teeth. Michael gave me a look that made me feel like I was Attila the Hun, out to end his precious life. (I also took away his hidden stash of mints—how mean was that?) But the truth was, I had my son's best interests in mind, as painful as it seemed to him at the time.

I had my son's best interests in mind, as painful as it seemed to him at the time.

Pain can be a gift. Whenever I go to my doctor with an ache or pain, he asks me, "Where does it hurt?" When I tell him my symptoms, he can diagnose what's going on and recommend a course of action. Pain was the gift that revealed there was trouble going on in my body; it was my signal to get some help. The pain was never really the problem, the problem was the problem; the pain just alerted me to the problem; it brought it to my attention.

Dr. Paul Brand is famous for his work among lepers. Leprosy is one of those diseases people don't like to talk about. This is because when leprosy goes untreated, the patient experiences horrible disfigurement: noses of leprosy patients shrink away; they lose fingers and toes, then hands and feet; many go blind. In his work with lepers, Dr. Brand discovered that it was not the disease of leprosy that caused the patient's flesh to deteriorate—

at least not directly. Their disfigurement was actually the result of their *not feeling pain*. Lepers, it turns out, destroy themselves unwittingly. They step on pieces of glass and don't feel it. They break a toe or scrape off their skin down to the bone without so much as a twinge of pain.

> It turns out that pain, at times, is a good thing.

Dr. Brand tells a horrifying story that captures this problem. One day he arrived at one of the leprosaria in India to do a group clinic. His visit had been announced in advance, and when the administrators of the camp rang the bell to get the patients' attention, a large group of lepers quickly began to move to the area where the clinic was being held.

Dr. Brand noticed one young patient emerging from the crowd. He was trying to beat the rest of them to the tent. At first he struggled across the edge of the courtyard with his crutches, holding his bandaged left leg clear of the ground. But as some other patients began to get ahead of him, he decided to race. As Dr. Brand watched, this young man tucked his crutches under his arm and began running. He ended up near the head of the line where he stood panting, leaning on his crutches, and sporting a huge smile of triumph.

The doctor knew from the odd way the man had been running that something was seriously wrong. As he walked toward the patient to investigate, Dr. Brand saw that his bandages were wet with blood and his left foot flopped freely from side to side. By running on an already dislocated ankle, the man had put far too much force on the end of his leg bone and had ripped away the flesh under the stress. He had no clue that he was running on the end of his tibia bone! As Dr. Brand knelt beside the man, he found that small stones and twigs had jammed through the end of the bone into the marrow cavity. He had no choice but to amputate the leg just below the knee.[12]

It turns out that pain, at times, is a good thing.

This belief has its roots in the teachings of St. Irenaeus and other early church leaders from the first and second century. They saw the presence of pain as something critical to the ongoing process of creation and therefore a backhanded *good*.

St. Irenaeus believed that our humanness was the raw material for a further and more difficult stage of God's creative work within us, the infusion of God's glory. God's dream was that this infusion would allow us to move into an even higher level of life (eternal life). God, from the beginning, had every intention of making more of us than mere human beings with only a natural, animal-like life to live. Irenaeus held that human beings need to participate in a transition from one level of existence, that of animal life (*bios*), to another and higher level of eternal life (*zoe*). This higher level includes but transcends the first. Peter said something similar when he wrote that we humans were designed to "participate in the divine nature."[13] We were destined to become *more* than physical beings.

St. Irenaeus believed that our humanness was the raw material for a further and more difficult stage of God's creative work within us.

We transition to being more spiritual than animal as we pursue a relationship with God *in the midst of hardships and pain*. How we face temptation and trouble determines whether *zoe* dawns in us or whether we live like mere men without the life of God. According to Irenaeus, pain helps form us. Either we give way to fear in the midst of the rough-and-tumble, or we call out to God to help us overcome. When we choose to run to God for the power of the Spirit, we experience the infusion of the divine life (*zoe*). This, according to Irenaeus, is God's aim for the human race; this is "the bringing of many sons to glory."

For Irenaeus, the dawning of *zoe* was not a given; it was neither natural nor inevitable. It was only experienced when a person chose a relationship with the living God. We may be fully human, but we are not fully imbued with divine life. Irenaeus proposed that planet Earth has always contained the possibility of evil by virtue of its being *unfinished*. But it was the human choice of rejecting God's life (the Fall) that made matters worse than they needed to be. Because of the Fall, the earth became filled with more trouble and heartache than its mere unfinished state necessitated. However, mortal humans still had the opportunity to be fashioned into moral, spiritual human beings through their unscripted responses to God's grace. This was the only path to becoming a child of God.

Irenaeus asserted that God's chief aim for humanity was not happiness, but development. His supreme and overriding goal for this planet was not to make it a place of pleasure without the pain. Rather, his goal was to make this a world for soul making. God, like any good parent, doesn't want us to view pleasure and happiness as our supreme value. Children committed to pleasure and happiness do not grow up as responsible adults (although they make excellent third-world dictators!). God is not against pleasure, but he is more interested in our developing moral integrity and a capacity for love,

Irenaeus asserted that God's chief aim for humanity was not happiness, but development.

as well as traits like humility, unselfishness, compassion, courage, and the like. He knows it is character, not things and circumstances, that makes us happy.

>>BUT WHAT ABOUT TRUE EVIL?

While I can buy in to the idea that sometimes pain is a gift—although it is a gift most people don't want—to say that *all* pain is good would be insane. Some suffering is fully evil, and to call it good is inconceivable. Moral evils like genocide, murder, and rape and natural evils like tsunamis and earthquakes are merciless, soul-destroying, life-ending evils. How could God ever allow these?

Unfortunately, the "no pain, no gain" view doesn't address this question. It leaves evil in the domain of mystery. It doesn't tell us why it is here or exactly how it got here or what role Satan plays in it. It only tells us that evil *is* here, and that it is part of this soul-making world.

The *unde malum?* (whence evil?) question has troubled theologians and philosophers for thousands of years. Early Christian thinkers influenced by a philosophy known as Gnosticism tried to solve the riddle of the *unde malum* by suggesting there must have been two gods: a good God (God Almighty) and an evil entity who was his counterpart. On this view, the tension between good and evil is a war between these two deities. But the church as a whole rejected this view. (Some Christians inadvertently still lean this way by giving Satan too much credit for all the evil that happens on the planet. He certainly plays a role, which we'll return to below, but it is not as grand a one as these folks suggest.)

>>THE ORIGINAL-SIN VIEW

The classic Christian view of the origin of evil has been most influenced by St. Augustine (354–430). This view has dominated Western Christianity (both Catholic and Protestant). Augustine claimed that in the beginning God created a perfect world that was good. Evil did not exist. This understanding is based on the early verses in Genesis which say of God's creative activity, "it was good."[14] Augustine believed that creation started *ex nihilo*—that things came out of nothing. Then God added order to what came into existence until it became something good. So the creative event went like this: something appears out of nothing and enters chaos ("without form, and void"[15]); then God adds order to the thing in chaos ("And God said, 'Let there be . . . '"[16]). Once the thing is ordered, God calls the thing "very good."[17]

Augustine asserted that because God is wholly good, he is only capable of creating good. Scripture echoes this by declaring that anything that "is good is from God,"[18] and that only the gifts that are "good and perfect" come "from above."[19] This means God is not the author of the ills in the world. He does not send tornadoes, earthquakes, tsunamis, and plagues. He doesn't cause car accidents or give folks cancerous brain tumors. In fact, anything that is *un*good does not come from God. Why? Because God is *only* good.

Which still leaves the question: whence evil?

Augustine tried to resolve this question by suggesting that evil appeared when sin fractured the good that was created. Something about sin ruined or pushed creation back toward disorder and chaos, thus reversing the wonderful trajectory of creation.

Sin was a kind of *anti*creation that pushed the good world God created into disorder, back into chaos heading directly for *ex nihilo*—nothingness! This *anti*creation tore apart and destroyed the good. This, for Augustine, was the origin of evil. Evil is good undone; it is a *direction,* the direction of *anti*creation. In this view, evil isn't a thing at all; it is the paling or destruction of the good God created.

Sin was a kind of *anti*creation that pushed the good world God created into disorder.

We can better understand Augustine's view by thinking of it this way: There are degrees of heat from little to smoldering hot, but there is no such thing as cold. Even absolute zero (-459.67 F degrees below zero) is the absence of heat, not the presence of cold. Cold isn't a thing. If it were, you would be able to add more of it and make things colder than absolute zero. But you can't. Cold is only a word we use to describe heat's absence. It is not heat's counterpart.

Evil, then, was not created. It is not the counterpart of good. Nor can things be created as evil. Created things are *only* good, and they can only become *less* good (evil). "Evil" is the description of the process of good things being destroyed. Total evil would simply be the complete absence of good.

So, *unde malum?* How did evil get here? Augustine said evil erupted on Earth because of human disobedience. However, Augustine did not mean that each individual person is responsible for the bad things that happen to him or her individually. He believed Adam's and Eve's choices to sin introduced a brokenness into the human race that gave evil a footing within the whole human family. But this brokenness extended beyond the human race and found a place in all of creation. The apostle Paul said it this way, "Here it is in a nutshell. . . . [Adam] did it wrong and got us in all this trouble with sin and death."[20] According to Augustine, this "original sin" is the reason for the brokenness and craziness of both moral and natural evils in the world.

But Augustine's schema doesn't explain why God allowed this to happen. And in the final analysis, the Bible never answers the question. Evil just inexplicably is. We know God didn't create it, but that's all that we know.

So where does Satan fit into the whole scheme of evil? Scripture never tells us how or why he ends up in the garden to tempt Adam and Eve with evil, but we do know that evil was first found in Satan before it ever appeared in the human race.[21] To suggest that Satan invented evil or masterminds its activity in the world is false; he is not that powerful. Certainly he engages in evil deeds and schemes, but he uses evil like a murderer misuses a gun. The murderer isn't necessarily the manufacturer of the gun, nor is he in control of every incident where guns are misused in the world.

To suggest that Satan invented evil or masterminds its activity in the world is false; he is not that powerful.

All we know biblically is that Satan is directly responsible for some evil acts and inspires people to act in evil ways (temptation). In the book of Job, Satan was the responsible party behind a tornado, the loss of life and property (with its resulting poverty), and the severe illness of Job. While Satan is not responsible for *all* bad weather or *all* sickness, obviously he is for some. God has also been known to mess with the weather[22] and to send illness as a judgment;[23] but that doesn't mean he is responsible for *all* bad weather or *all* illness either. The more you try to understand evil, the more you discover it is a notoriously tricky enterprise, full of multilayered complexity.

Jesus once mentioned a tower falling on a group of tourists around Jerusalem,[24] but he never said anything about God or Satan being involved—it appears to have been the result of bad construction. Apparently, the humans who built the tower were responsible for that horror. Also, Paul claimed that the planet itself is "groaning" in pain and experiencing chaos all on its own—apart from God, Satan, or human effort.[25] This is also part of the why behind radical weather and catastrophic planetary changes, as well as animal pain and suffering, the harshness and emptiness of the universe, and so on.

There are some legitimate gripes about all this. No matter how evil came into the world, isn't God (like any responsible parent) still responsible on some level for allowing it to happen? And if God is all-powerful, why doesn't he just fix it? Or why doesn't he at least stop the seemingly undeserved or soul-destroying suffering that involves children, the elderly, or those who are helpless? And will evil ever be stopped?

Lots of questions. Disturbing ones.

>>THE "GOD IS IN CONTROL" VIEW

Many Christians today hold that everything that happens is predestined, or it wouldn't happen. The implication of this is: you can't change stuff. What is, is for some purpose. This view is rooted in the philosophy of determinism, a fatalistic position. It actually came from a group known as the Epicureans (300 B.C.) who held to the idea that life is invariably predetermined. They reasoned that since we can change nothing, we might as well float through life. "Don't worry; be happy" was their credo (before Bobby McFerrin ever sang it). Why get perturbed about things you can't change? They doled out the original chill pill. This view was extremely popular in the premodern world. Why?

It is hard for us moderns to appreciate the harshness of the ancient world. Life was cruel. War, death, plagues, exploding volcanoes, illness, bad teeth (with no modern dentists or Tylenol) were givens for those living in that day. Even with herculean effort, simple things like having shelter and daily food were beyond the grasp of the average person. People died young. In this kind of world, simply holding up through one's suffering was an amazing feat. People were focused on surviving from one day (or hour) to the next. In this kind of helter-skelter, bump-and-roll habitat, the philosophy of determinism gave people hope that *something* was in charge, though they had no hope of ever changing that something. So, since you can't control anything, don't get your hopes up about anything . . . just chill. It was a seductive view that gave folks an emotional and intellectual handle with which to process the harshness of a premodern, pretechnological existence.

The Epicureans reasoned that since we can change nothing, we might as well float through life.

When Christianity came on the scene, it stood in stark contrast to the pagan philosophy of determinism. The idea of grace brought hope to humanity, hope that things *can* change. Grace is God getting in the mix of the average person's world, and as a result, favor and good come into that person's life. When favor and good come, they foster positive and progressive change. *Things can be different!* This was the message of Christianity. We don't have to accept what is; we can trust God to transform people and cultures. No fatalistic determinism here.

But then, in the 1500s, the Reformation came along. During this period determinism found its way smack into Christian theology under the banner of the doctrine of God's sovereignty. The Reformation scholars tackled the issue of evil by claiming God uses it in mysterious ways, which is another way of saying, *Just shut up and take it.* This view is best caught by the joke: What does a five-hundred-pound gorilla do? Punch line: Anything he wants to. The Reformers believed that God manages everything that happens in this world, including evil. After all, he's the one with all the power. The concept of sovereignty became so radicalized that people came to believe that God predetermined whether people go to heaven or hell, even before they arrived on the planet at birth! This was not the historical, orthodox, biblical teaching concerning God's sovereignty; this was sovereignty on steroids.

This view became so pervasive in the West that insurance companies have now picked up on the idea and call all the bad stuff—hurricanes, earthquakes, floods, and tornadoes—*acts of God.* I guess those were just bad-God days. This idea fosters boring, oversimplified, religious drivel like: "Everything happens for a reason."

Que Será, Será

The problem with an overemphasis on God's sovereignty is that you end up with a kind of "Que será, será" theology rather than a biblical one. Some of you may remember the old song performed by Doris Day. The chorus goes:

Que será, será,
Whatever will be, will be.
The future's not ours to see,
Que será, será.[26]

People who buy into radicalized sovereignty believe that whatever is to be will be. They contend that we have nothing to do with the future; that is God's sphere. For these folks, prayer is more of an aside, because God will do what God will do. Things only happen because of God's sovereignty, and human beings don't really cause anything to happen through prayer that God wouldn't have done anyway. Therefore, one should pray only to accept what God does, not to change it. Faith to such a believer is nothing more than agreement with what is already determined to be.

The problem with an overemphasis on God's sovereignty is that you end up with a kind of "Que será, será" theology rather than a biblical one.

Admittedly, the Bible does hold that this is true in some cases. For example, when the Jewish religious leaders tried to stop the momentum of the burgeoning infant Christian movement, one of their number wisely said, "So I am telling you: Hands off these men! Let them alone. If this program or this work is merely human, it will fall apart, but if it is of God, there is nothing you can do about it—and you better not be found fighting against God!"[27] There are some "God things" we can do nothing about. They are just going to happen. Paul said God "works out everything in agreement with the counsel and design of His [own] will."[28] He also wrote, "Who in the world do you think you are to second-guess God? Do you for one moment suppose any of us knows enough to call God into question? Clay doesn't talk back to the fingers that mold it, saying, 'Why did you shape me like this?'"[29] Some of what God does *is* backed up by his sovereignty; we must accept those things.

But the Bible is also jammed with story after story of God responding to the will of his people. Once, as Jesus walked through a crowd, a sick woman snuck up to him and touched the hem of his garment. The Bible says, "Jesus realized that power had gone out from him."[30] The woman was instantly healed. Jesus stopped to investigate. When the woman came forward, trembling and admitting she had touched him, he said something amazing. He told her that her faith initiated the miracle. Think of that. A human being initiated an action of God!

Paul said God performs acts "prompted" by our faith.[31] John boldly declared that "everyone born of God overcomes the world" and that "this is the victory that overcomes the world, even our faith."[32] This suggests that not everything God does is an expression of his sovereignty. Even a casual reading of Scripture points to the idea that when we trust and pray, things happen that don't happen if we don't do these things.

The Bible is jammed with story after story of God responding to the will of his people.

The Old Testament tells the story of a prophet who told the people facing an overwhelming army that they would "not have to fight this battle."[33] He said there would be no casualties; God was going to fight for them. And he did. Another time an Israelite leader stood up as they faced a terrifying army and said, "Do not be afraid. Stand firm and you will see the deliverance the Lord will bring you today." But God replied, "Why are you crying out to me?" and commanded the leader and the people to engage and do some things for themselves.[34] Sometimes God does it all; other times we have a role to play.

Is Anything Up to Us?

What, then, is up to us? Is there anything contingent upon our actions? What rules or controls our lives here or in the hereafter? When we consider these haunting questions, we are trying to get our minds around whether God's involvement with us is predetermined—free from the influence of our human will. These questions have beguiled theologians and philosophers for eons, and I am not about to say anything profound enough to settle them here, but perhaps that is the point. Perhaps some things are determined and some are not, some things are destined to be and some are not. Maybe we need wisdom and humility to discern which things fit where.

God's sovereignty changed in response to a human action.

Take death, for example. The Bible says everyone is going to die[35]—unless you are part of the group that is living when Jesus comes back. There is no way out, the Sovereign One has spoken. Yet the Bible claims there are things you can do to add length to your life, such as loving God's Word.[36] An old, sick king named Hezekiah was told by a big-time, always-right prophet that he was going to die. The prophet then left the king's house. Meanwhile, Hezekiah was bawling his eyes out, calling on God. God told the prophet, who had only gotten as far as the king's front yard, to go back and tell the king that God had just added fifteen years to his life![37] What was that all about? Somehow, God's sovereignty changed in response to a human action. Does free will play a role in death? Paul claimed he had a choice about the timing of his death.[38] I'm not suggesting this happens all the time, but it does happen sometimes, which means that, though death is determined, the timing sometimes isn't. *Wow.*

If death can be influenced by free will, then what about life? What about the quality of our marriages and our relationships with our kids, friends, and coworkers? What about our career successes or general well-being in life? How much do we control in all of this, and what does that control look like? How can we assert control without overstepping God's sovereignty? How can we know when things are to happen via sovereignty versus human will? More questions.

The radical-sovereignty crowd assumes evil is present in the world because God willed it to be so—that God has some purpose for it all. Some aspects of that view are seductive. "Maybe this is happening for something better to happen," we reason. And certainly there are verses that suggest that suffering evil can lead to something better. "And we know that in all things God works for the good of those who love him, who have been called according to his purpose."[39] But just because God can make good out of evil does not mean he sends the evil in order to get the good. Why would God *need* evil to bring good? I think many are confused about this and misread God's capacity to work "all things" (especially the bad things) into "good." They assume God sends the bad in order to bring the good. However, what if God is so good he actually reverses the

Just because God can make good out of evil does not mean he sends the evil in order to get the good.

direction of evil, and good begins to emerge—not *because* of the evil, but *in spite* of it?

>>WHY?

Though these thoughts help me to not want to jump ship on my faith, they do little for me in the face of pain. I still don't get why God just doesn't abort evil and pain here and now. Why doesn't he just appear with power and work whatever miracles he needs to work in order to wipe away every tear, calm every storm, right every wrong, and make beautiful everything that is now ugly? The Scripture claims he will do that someday[40]—but someday is not today. I wish it were today. I don't get why he is waiting.

I don't get why evil is so hard to explain. Why can't God show us the direct cause-and-effect reasons evil appears in the world? Then we could work to stop it once and for all. But simple, cause-and-effect evaluations just don't hold up. Evil just isn't that simple to explain.

However, letting go of my quest to understand evil is not an easy thing for me to do. I do well when things are going well, but then the evil day comes and I sit stupefied. Any attempt at theodicy—trying to explain the why behind the evil or trying to hope for a better tomorrow—becomes a waste of time. In the face of devastating loss, there is no sense in saying "tomorrow." History stops. The more intense the evil, the more faith seems like a useless commodity. After all, the faith I had before the evil appeared didn't prevent it; why would it do me any good now? Faith appears bankrupt. In this context, at best, faith seems irrelevant. At worst, it trivializes the suffering.

There is no way to grasp evil—no way to make any of it intelligible. How can one overlook the raw, concrete pain and try to explain it? Why would you try? It would be nothing but an abstraction. It certainly does nothing to lessen the pain. Yet, I choose to run to God. Why? Because no matter what I see or experience, I believe God is good. Call it naïveté. But I have discovered that, in some strange way, running to God—when everything in me wants to run from him and to judge him—actually begins the process of overcoming evil. I have discovered in the context of living and working with communities of faith numbering in the thousands that, though evil cannot be completely halted by faith, somehow faith begins to take the sting and pain out of evil and unleashes waves of good into our lives. So much so that there are times when people look back on their pain, and it ends up seeming it was "good" that the "evil" showed up in their lives! (We'll return to this crazy idea shortly.)

Somehow faith begins to take the sting and pain out of evil and unleashes waves of good into our lives.

>>IN SPITE OF EVIL

As I said above, the Bible never answers the question, *whence evil?* Evil just is, and God did not create it. Not very satisfying, I know. Yet the Bible says much about how God works for our good *in spite of* evil. I've discovered that whenever a person ponders those biblical claims, hope dawns—no matter how devastating the evil may be. There are a number of ways that God acts in the face of evil. Let's look at three: he acts *as a friend*; he acts *with a call*; he acts *as a Judge.*

As a Friend

I got the call at 1:00 a.m. the night that Tim and Janet's child was killed in the car accident. I raced to the hospital, and as I was about to get out of my car, I felt sick. I didn't want to go in—I was afraid to go in. Something in us wants to run from pain and suffering, and this was any parent's nightmare come true.

No one had to tell me where the family was. I just followed the sound of the heart-wrenching sobs and screaming cries. As I entered the room, they were in each other's arms, crying uncontrollably. I went over and put my hands on their shoulders. As they glanced up to see me, they turned to hug and to push out the words through their hiccuped sobs, "Our baby . . . she's gone." It was a devastating moment. I didn't know what to say; I felt completely helpless. But somehow my being there, saying nothing, doing nothing, was important to them—they told me so. I needed to simply *be there*.

As trite as it may sound at first blush, God's initial response to the pain in our world is to come *to us* in our pain. Remember, in the Fall of humankind we chose to push away from God. But instead of abandoning us, he chose to stay with us. And not just with those who are believers. God watches every human being on this planet and is touched by everything that touches every person. Jesus told folks, "Not a single sparrow can fall to the ground without your Father knowing it. And the very hairs on your head are all numbered. So don't be afraid; you are more valuable to God than a whole flock of sparrows."[41] God pays attention to our lives.

God's initial response to the pain in our world is to come *to us* in our pain.

Catherine Marshall wrote:

> If we are to believe Jesus, his Father and our Father is the God of all life, and his caring and provision include a sheepherder's lost lamb, a falling sparrow, a sick child, the hunger pangs of a crowd of four thousand, the need for wine at a wedding feast, and the plight of professional fishermen who toiled all night and caught nothing. These vignettes, scattered through the Gospels like little patches of gold dust, say to us. "No creaturely need is outside the scope or range of prayer." In other words, *God cares about whatever we care about and is touched by whatever touches us.*[42]

You are not broken without him being broken. You are not rejected without him tasting your rejection. You do not face fears that he does not face along with you.

Incarnation is God embracing all the agony and all the pain of this world.

God cares. He certainly doesn't have to. He had every justification for abandoning the human race. Yet God comes to us, the ones who turned away from him. You want to know the answer to *Where is God?* when a child is dying or starving, or when an earthquake has trapped thousands under debris, or when a brain cancer has ravaged a young mother of three? He is *with them* in their agony and pain. Every tear is his tear; every heartbreak is his heartbreak. Jesus Christ came to this planet in order to enter the pain of the Fall. Theologians call it The Incarnation—it is God embracing all the agony and all the pain of this world. And this gesture of taking on our pain is the most impressive sign of God's love for us, even more so than God using his power to stop the pain!

Somehow knowing God is *with us* dulls the sharp pain of evil.

No matter how hopeless things become, Jesus is there, sitting beside us in the darkest places of our lives. Somehow knowing God is *with us* dulls the sharp pain of evil. St. Teresa of Avila said, "In the light of heaven, the worst suffering on earth, a life full of the most atrocious tortures on earth, will be seen to be no more serious than one night in an inconvenient hotel."

Even in the face of death—the "last enemy to be destroyed,"[43] which is the endgame of evil, God is present. Listen to these words from a letter found by archeologists from a first-century martyr:

> In a dark hole I have found cheerfulness; in a place of bitterness and death I have found rest. While others weep I have found laughter, where others fear I have found strength. Who would believe that in a state of misery I have had great pleasure; that in a lonely corner I have had glorious company and in the hardest of bonds perfect repose. All those things Jesus has granted me. He is with me, comforts me and fills me with joy. He drives bitterness from me and fills me with strength and consolation.[44]

We live in a broken world. Jesus was honest with us and told us that this is a place filled with trouble.[45] God's first response is simply coming to us. He listens to us and becomes one with us in our pain; he enters it with us. That may sound like a sappy and weak response to evil, but just wait till your world is rocked.

You will be surprised at how consoling and hopeful it is to know that Jesus Christ is with you when you hear that doctor's report or suffer an unexpected loss. His presence will be exactly what you want.

That may sound like a sappy and weak response to evil, but just wait till your world is rocked.

With a Call

Another way God acts in the face of evil is *with a call* to his people to fight against that evil. Paul tells us exactly what to fight evil with: "Do not be overcome by evil, but overcome evil with good."[46] Remember, evil is the undoing of good; it is *anti*creation. As Christ followers, we are to attack the evil we encounter with good works. Jesus said, "Let your light shine before men, that they may see your good deeds and praise your Father in heaven."[47] These "good things" don't earn us eternal favor from God, they give us an edge over evil in this world. We are to engage in good works to overcome evil. This is how we—the members of Christ's body—are to respond to the evil we encounter in this world. We must get involved. Jesus told a story about the last judgment that is worth looking at here:

> When he finally arrives, blazing in beauty and all his angels with him, the Son of Man will take his place on his glorious throne. Then all the nations will be arranged before him and he will sort the people out, much as a shepherd sorts out sheep and goats, putting sheep to his right and goats to his left.
>
> Then the King will say to those on his right, "Enter, you who are blessed by my Father! Take what's coming

to you in this kingdom. It's been ready for you since the world's foundation. And here's why:

> I was hungry and you fed me,
> I was thirsty and you gave me a drink,
> I was homeless and you gave me a room,
> I was shivering and you gave me clothes,
> I was sick and you stopped to visit,
> I was in prison and you came to me.

Then those "sheep" are going to say, "Master, what are you talking about? When did we ever see you hungry and feed you, thirsty and give you a drink? And when did we ever see you sick or in prison and come to you?" Then the King will say, "I'm telling the solemn truth: Whenever you did one of these things to someone overlooked or ignored, that was me—you did it to me."[48]

Two things in this story are worth pointing out. First, notice that Jesus said he has so identified with the pain of humanity that when someone is hungry, he is; when someone is thirsty, he is; when someone is homeless, he is; when someone is cold or naked or sick or imprisoned, he is. Second, notice that he expects his people to do something about these evils, not just tell those touched by pain to pray for miracles to eliminate their hunger, thirst, homelessness, sickness, and so on. He expects us to shower these folks with acts of kindness and good works, believing that when we do things for them, we are doing them for Jesus himself! It turns out that we really are our brother's keeper.

We often wonder why God allows poverty, famine, and injustice in the first place, when he could do something about it. Maybe we need to stop and consider that God may be wondering why *we* don't do something about it. What if we are to take on Jesus' heart toward suffering and hurting people and do what we can to alleviate suffering wherever we see it? Maybe one reason there is so much evil on this planet is because Christ followers have failed to rise up and do something about it. Perhaps the church has become, as the old adage says, so heavenly minded, we are of no earthly good.

We need to stop and consider that God may be wondering why *we* don't do something about it.

I think we have failed here. I know I have. It's time for us to repent and engage. This means we need to look for pain in our world—and there is much. It might be the look of dread in a waitress's eyes or a coworker going through a personal struggle. We could also research the social needs in the cities in which we live and then find and support organizations that are working to eliminate those needs. Organizations such as the American Red Cross, the One Campaign, or World Relief make getting involved easy. The organization doesn't even have to be overtly Christian to be worth becoming involved with. Just helping people is a dream of God's and should be ours. Besides, if you are a Christian full of light, you will bring Christ with you into whatever you participate in, and then that activity is "Christian."

I just ran across an article in the *Wall Street Journal*[49] about a retired gentleman by the name of Mark Goldsmith, a former executive at Revlon and Shiseido, who has found a new calling: working in prison. Mr. Goldsmith, along with fourteen other retired executives, works at GOSO (Getting Out and Staying

Out), a nonprofit education organization he started in 2005. GOSO is working with 275 inmates serving time in Upstate New York prisons, plus an additional 150 at Rikers. GOSO, which is based in Harlem, works to break the repeat-offender story where young men get released from prison without skills, jobs, money, or a place to live, only to resort to crime that lands them back in jail again. Of the 400 inmates GOSO has worked with since its inception, fewer than 10 percent of them have been rearrested (the annual percentage of prisoners being rearrested after being released is closer to 66 percent nationally). These retired men spend several days a week at the prisons, counseling and encouraging the teens to keep working on their high-school equivalency diplomas. They use the same motivational techniques they used to grow their successful businesses when they were in the work force.

These ex-CEOs provide individual job and education coaching and maintain a job bank of openings with employers willing to hire former prisoners and give educational scholarships. These retirees may be done in the work force, but they were not done living. What a great way to eliminate evil and visit "Jesus" while he is in prison.

I also think there needs to be a fresh commitment of young people in the church to enter higher education. From economics to medicine to social justice, believers should be digging in their heels, learning all they can, and praying as they research ways to overcome poverty, disease, and social injustice wherever they are found. Yes, we are to preach Christ, but why not do so as we work to eliminate whatever evil we can? What if crippling poverty, needless starvation, and much of the illness in the world are here—not because God allows it—but because we do?

As a Judge

While it may appear that evil people get away with evil, don't be fooled. God isn't letting evil perpetrators get away with evil. Though he forgives those who repent, people who continue to reject God and push evil agendas will answer to God. From our human perspective, it may look as if they are getting away with it, but we are only on this planet for a hundred years or so. God doesn't feel the pressure to demonstrate his justice to us; he calls us to trust that he is fair and just. There will come a day when he will settle accounts and hold people accountable for the evil and suffering they've caused.

Justice delayed is *not* justice denied. God is the Author and Creator of time, and he can take whatever time he wants to finish the story he is writing. But one thing is certain: he will resolve all that needs to be resolved by the time his plot comes to a close.

>>DARE TO TRUST GOD

The skeptic still cries, "If God exists and he is good, then why would he allow evil and suffering in the world?" And the truth is, I wish I knew. But I don't. Nobody does. However, I still dare to trust that God is good. His choosing to come to us in the midst of our pain and suffering, his call for his people to fight evil and overcome it with good, and his commitment to judge what needs to be judged all demonstrate his deep commitment to eventually overcome the evil that is in this world.

The Bible records a day, at the end of the age when all evil and its results will be abolished. John wrote:

Then I saw a new heaven and a new earth, for the first heaven and the first earth had passed away, and there was no longer any sea. I saw the Holy City, the new Jerusalem, coming down out of heaven from God, prepared as a bride beautifully dressed for her husband. And I heard a loud voice from the throne saying, "Now the dwelling of God is with men, and he will live with them. They will be his people, and God himself will be with them and be their God. He will wipe every tear from their eyes. There will be no more death or mourning or crying or pain, for the old order of things has passed away."[50]

I long for that day.

04

>>A LONE SAVIOR

it bothers me that Jesus is the only way to a relationship with God

"I think everyone has to find his own spiritual path to God," my fellow shopper said.

I don't remember how we got on the subject of finding God. He may have asked me what I did for a living and I told him I was a pastor. At any rate, we were in a deep spiritual conversation in the fairly long checkout line at Best Buy.

"Wouldn't that be cool if it were true?" I responded.

"What do you mean?" he queried.

"It would be great if everyone could find his or her own spiritual path to God," I answered. "But that's not what Jesus said would happen. He claimed there was only *one* path and that no one can get to God except through him."[1]

Whenever I get in a spiritual conversation with someone, a part of me cringes as I talk about the exclusive claims of Jesus Christ. I love Jesus, and I have come to believe his claims, but that doesn't mean I don't struggle with the idea that Christianity doesn't allow for the position that each person can find his or her own path to God. It seems to me that if a person is open to spiritual reality in general, that should be enough. After all, isn't Jesus big enough and gracious enough to allow all religious impulses and thoughts to ultimately lead back to him? Surely open-mindedness, humility, and liberality fit into the Christian ethic, so why not into Christian theology? Why can't faith be this open?

>>EVERYTHING ELSE IS RELATIVE

Unless you have been living in a bunker for the past thirty years, like Brendan Fraser in *Blast from the Past,* you know that we are living in a world of relativism. *Relativism* is the belief that all points of view are equally valid: what *you* think is right and wrong is right and wrong for you, and what *I* think is right and wrong is right and wrong for me. Though our lists may be different, our lists are equally legitimate.

There is something very seductive about this view. If a thing is right just because I think it is, then being right is an easy proposition. Being able to select one's own right and wrong fuels a sense of personal empowerment. It means I can do whatever I want to do. And if that isn't freedom, it certainly feels like freedom. You can see how this perspective would help us to stop judging one another and begin respecting one another's personal convictions. Why wouldn't we? Relativism fosters the sense that everyone is right, which delivers personal empowerment, the debunking of judgment, and a respect for others and their opinions. These are all good things, right?

Of course, this view also means there are no absolutes, no truth that is true for everyone—just relative ideas that are true to *each* one. What's good for me is not necessarily good for you, and vice versa. Thus, everyone must find his or her own way. This view engenders a sense of unity in matters of faith, because what you believe about God and what I believe about God are equally good and equally true. We can stop focusing on *what* one believes and applaud all belief in general, because all paths lead to God. Who wouldn't love that?

Rabbi Shmuley Boteach echoes the cry of many in our day who are against religious feuding when he states, "I am absolutely against any religion that says that one faith is superior to another. I don't see how that is anything different than spiritual racism. It's a way of saying that we are closer to God than you, and that's what leads to hatred."[2]

As appealing as relativism is, and while the intellectually elite and culturally *en vogue* espouse that it is the only tenable position, it doesn't appear to be an option for the Christ follower. Why? Because the claims of Christ are absolute and universal. Jesus claimed to be "the way and the truth and the life," and that "no one comes to the Father" except through him.[3]

>>THE PROBLEM WITH TRUTH

The problem with the concept of truth is that it is exclusive by nature. Any time a person makes a truth claim, he or she is saying all other contradictory claims are false. Hence, truth is nonnegotiable; it is stark and raw. For example, the notion that Earth is orbiting the sun is either true or it is not. There is no room for negotiating, though it seems as if the sun is orbiting around the

Truth has no interest in what I think or feel about the matter; subjective views are irrelevant.

earth from *my* perspective. Truth has no interest in what I think or feel about the matter; subjective views are irrelevant.

If truth exists, then there are people who are right and people who are wrong. But we don't like that. It's too judgmental. Consequently, two-thirds of Americans now deny there's any such thing as truth.[4] We prefer opinion to truth. It's more civilized.

Yet, as a Christ follower, I'm faced with the challenge that Christianity is not just presented as another subjective, religious philosophy. Christians see the claims of Jesus Christ as *objectively true*—true in the sense that gravity is true. And if the gospel of Jesus Christ is truth, then it is absolute and true for all people. The problem is, there are so many knotty and untenable implications with that position.

At first blush Christ's claims seem to smack of arrogance, bigotry, and narrow-mindedness. And, in a cultural milieu that holds pluralism and tolerance sacrosanct, claiming that Jesus of Nazareth is the only path to God is met with great resistance. Pluralist Rosemary Radford Ruether labeled this as "absurd religious chauvinism,"[5] while another religious leader called it a "spiritual dictatorship"[6] that encourages smug superiority and unnecessary judgment. All of us have witnessed the hatred and violence that comes from religious one-upping. As a culture, we are much more accepting of comments like that of Indian philosopher Swami Vivekenanda who said, "By the study of different religions we find that in essense they are one."[7] He claimed the real sin was to call someone else a sinner.

At first blush Christ's claims seem to smack of arrogance, bigotry, and narrow-mindedness.

The claim that Jesus is the only way to God is hard to accept when you consider that 840 million people believe "there is no

God but God, and Muhammad is his prophet"; that 650 million Hindus accept the Vedas and the Upanishads as sacred and look forward to Nirvana; that multiple millions accept the teachings of the Buddha, Confucius, and Lao-tse and have no knowledge of the teachings of Jesus.

In the light of this, I honestly don't know what to do with these arguments against Christian absolutism. And, truth be told, on some level I struggle here. How *can* it be possible that so many have it so wrong? And what of those sincere souls who never have the opportunity to hear about Jesus Christ? Will they really go to hell?

I wish I could tell you that I have all this resolved in my mind. I don't. The wrestling match continues to this day. The only solace I have found is that I believe that God is good and that God is fair. Though it may sound like an intellectual cop-out, something in me finds rest in the promise of God's goodness and fairness—like young children who trust that all will be well just because they are with their father or mother.

That being said, there is much inclusiveness in Christian thought about how God is working in the lives of every person everywhere—even when the person doesn't immediately recognize him. And there is biblical evidence that supports the idea that there is a loophole for those who have not heard the message of the gospel (see below)! These ideas may not assuage all that bothers me about this issue, but they do help.

>>PREGOSPEL GOD FOLLOWERS

Richard Wurmbrand, author of *Tortured for Christ*, wrote of a Russian officer who was a God-follower without knowing anything about Jesus:

This man came to me. He loved God, he longed after God, but he had never seen a Bible. He never attended religious services. He had no religious education. He loved God without the slightest knowledge of him.

I read to him the Sermon on the Mount and the parables of Jesus. After hearing them, he danced around the room in rapturous joy proclaiming "What a wonderful beauty! How could I live without knowing this Christ!"

Then I made a mistake, I read to him the passion and crucifixion of Christ. He had not expected it and, when he heard how Christ was beaten, how he was crucified, and that in the end he died, he fell in an armchair and began to weep bitterly. He had believed in a Savior and now his Savior was dead!

Then I read to him the story of the resurrection. When he heard this wonderful news, he beat his knees and swore a very dirty, but I think a very "holy" swear. This was his crude manner. He rejoiced and shouted for joy: "He is alive! He is alive!" Again he danced around the room, overwhelmed with happiness!

"O God, what a fine chap you are!"

He did not know how to pray our holy phrases. He fell on his knees together with me and his words of prayer were: "O God, what a fine chap you are! If I were you and you were me, I would *never* have forgiven you your sins. But you are really a very nice chap! I love you from all my heart!"[8]

When I read this, I couldn't help but get the feeling that God was at work in this Russian officer long before Reverend Wurmbrand ever met him. "Well," someone might ask, "was he *saved* before he understood the Savior and the gospel?" My evangelical theological tradition screams, "Absolutely not!" But, honestly, I don't know.

Paul suggested there is a loophole for those who have never heard the gospel.

Paul dealt with this riddle and suggested there is a loophole for those who have never heard the gospel when he wrote:

> When outsiders who have never heard of God's law follow it more or less by instinct, they confirm its truth by their obedience. They show that God's law is not something alien, imposed on us from without, but woven into the very fabric of our creation. There is something deep within them that echoes God's yes and no, right and wrong. Their response to God's yes and no will become public knowledge on the day God makes his final decision about every man and woman. The Message from God that I proclaim through Jesus Christ takes into account all these differences.[9]

>>A BUDDHIST CHRISTIAN?

Tony Campolo, in his book *Speaking My Mind*, tells a story that raises this same question. He writes:

> A leading evangelist told me about an encounter he had with a non-Christian during a trip through China.

While there, he visited the monastery, and as he entered the walled-in gardens of the place, he noticed one of the monks in deep meditation. At the prompting of the Spirit, he went over to talk to the man, and with his translator, he explained the story of Jesus. He opened the New Testament and showed him what the Bible taught about salvation. As he spoke, he noticed that the monk was visibly moved. Actually, there were tears in the monk's eyes. My friend, the evangelist, then said, "Won't you accept this Jesus into your heart and let him be your personal Savior?"

The monk answered with surprise, "Accept him? How can I accept him into my life when he is already there? All the time you were telling me about him, I heard his Spirit say, 'He is talking of me! He is talking of me!' I do not need to accept him. He is already in me, affirming the message of your Bible. I have known him for a long, long time."

My friend asked me, "Was this man possessed by Jesus before I ever arrived? Was he a Christian before he knew the name of Jesus? And, if I had not come with the gospel message, would God accept him on the Day of Judgment?"[10]

Questions. Uncomfortable ones, particularly for us evangelicals.

>>WHAT CHRISTIANITY IS NOT SAYING

Though the Christian's claim is that God is most clearly seen through the life and person of Jesus Christ, that does not mean God is absent from the lives of people who participate in other world religions. In fact, Christians should assume that God *is* moving in the life of every person, in every place, at all times. The Christian position is that God cares for all of us, but many misunderstand what is really going on. Let me explain.

I shared in an earlier chapter about the apostle Paul's visit to the city of Athens. It was full of idols and idol worship, and at first Paul was "greatly distressed."[11] You get the feeling that as he walked around, he was looking for something—it appeared that he was looking for evidence of God's kingdom in their midst. He ended up claiming that the Athenians were "very religious" because God was already at work in their culture. He pointed to an altar, which they had built to an "Unknown God," and said, "I'm here to introduce you to this God so you can worship intelligently, know who you're dealing with."[12]

Imagine that. Paul actually told the Athenians that God had always been with them—that he had even "determined the times set for them and the exact places where they should live."[13] This means God had destined them to be born in Athens, though it was not a Christian city. And Paul claimed God did this so people "would seek him" and "find him" because he was "not far from each one of [them]."[14] Paul even claimed that all the non-Christian Athenians were wrapped in God's care—*while they were worshiping false gods*—and he tells them: "In him we live and move and have our being."[15]

God was present in that culture before Paul got there with the gospel! But the gospel is the simplest and clearest way to reveal what God is up to.

God was present and working in that culture before Paul got there with the gospel! Although the gospel is the simplest and clearest way to reveal what God is up to, it does not have to be present for God to be working. The reason that Christians push back from other religions and call them false is not because God isn't involved with the people in those religions, but because their stories reinterpret real God events into false metanarratives (stories). Hence, the true God remains unknown to them.

A classic example of this occurred when Paul was visiting the city of Lystra and healed a crippled man in the name of Jesus. It was a miracle of God, but the crowds co-opted the healing event into their own familiar Greek mythological god story, claiming, "The gods have come down to us in human form!"[16] They thought Paul and his partner were the incarnated Greek gods Zeus and Hermes, and they completely missed the true God. Paul told them that the event had nothing to do with their false gods but was from the God who was revealed in Jesus Christ—the God who had always, in Paul's words, "shown kindness by giving you rain from heaven and crops in their seasons; he provides you with plenty of food and fills your hearts with joy."[17]

People's confusion does not preempt God from moving in their lives.

Paul didn't get mad at the crowds for ascribing to their false gods what the true God had done. He understood they were mixed up theologically. That is how Christians should look at those who live in other faith traditions. Christian tolerance must rule the day. The truth is, whether or not people get what is actually going on, God is still at work in every nation of the world, at every moment in human history, in every living man, woman, and child.

However, many co-opt God's work into the god stories they are familiar with—to the Hindu believer, God's kindnesses are believed to be the result of good karma; to the Native American, the Great Spirit must be pleased with them; to the Australian Aborigine, the demons must have been expelled; to the atheist, the good just "happened" because that's the way the world evolved to be. Is that what's really going on? No. But those outside of God's kingdom build "altars" out of the familiar order to describe the kindness of God they do not fully understand. What's wild to me is that people's confusion does not preempt God from moving in their lives—he is still there, working. He loves the world.

Paul saw his mission was to preach the gospel—a kind of decoder ring that would help people rightly interpret and appropriately respond to the working of God in their lives. The appropriate response, as laid out by the gospel, would be repentance and surrender to the lordship of Jesus Christ. In this context, Paul told those in Athens that God commands "all people everywhere to repent."[18] God wanted them to understand who he really was—that he was seen most clearly in Jesus of Nazareth.

Our job as Christ followers is to help people meet the Giver of all good, to help them experience his person, not just his kindness. Jesus prayed, "Now this is eternal life: that they may know you, the only true God, and Jesus Christ, whom you have sent."[19] Getting to "know" God through Jesus Christ is what causes personal transformation.

Getting to "know" God through Jesus Christ is what causes personal transformation.

People are not far away from God when they believe false things. He is right there with them; "in him we live and move."[20] Paul told the Athenians, "God did this so that men would seek him and perhaps reach out for him and find him, though he is not far from each one of us."[21] No Muslim or Hindu or atheist is far from God—God is right there within their reach! He is right there giving them all the good they know. They are just confused about it.

How would Christians approach others with the message of God if they thought this way? How would they approach their wayward children or relatives or Muslim neighbors? How would they share with those on the job who don't embrace Jesus? As a Christ follower, I may be "greatly distressed," as Paul was, when I survey the lives of those who are Christless. But I will look for where God is working in their lives and try to help them see it, rather than blowing them off and treating them dismissively because they don't know the truth. Maybe sharing Jesus with others is more about perspective than using a bullhorn to yell at people.

People are not far away from God when they believe false things. He is right there with them.

>>SOMETHING TO CONSIDER

In a pluralistic world we should expect folks to be bothered by the truth claim that Jesus is the only way, but this is only exacerbated by the arrogance many put forward when they believe they are right and others are wrong. Maybe it is the truthtellers' methodology that has given truth such a bad rap. Maybe truth would be more applauded if those who know it would be nicer about it. There is something in folks (dare I say in all of us?) that loves to place self above others, to appear better than others. Historically, Christians have been notorious for pushing Christ down people's throats in antagonistic, hostile, and even violent ways that are contrary to the love of Christ. How we assumed we could communicate the love of Jesus in nonloving ways is beyond anyone's ability to explain. Yet, Christ's church is guilty as charged.

Christian apologist Ravi Zacharias once said with a sigh, "If truth is not undergirded by love, it makes the possessor of that truth obnoxious and the truth repulsive." He went on to say that the Christian church has much to answer for in regards to our inappropriate methodology throughout history. "In India," he said, "we have a proverb that says once you cut off a person's nose, there's no point in giving him a rose to smell."[22]

The answer to this is found in the person of Christ as revealed in the Gospels. He welcomed all without judgment or rejection. The only ones Jesus rebuked were those full of themselves and those who propped themselves up as being better than everyone else. Jesus champions humankind and sides with the disenfranchised, the hurting, and the alienated. Though Jesus Christ embodies truth, he also embodies love. John wrote that in Christ there exists both "truth and love."[23] They don't have to be mutually exclusive. Because Jesus embodies both truth and love, people are open to Jesus. However, the same cannot be said for his followers. Mahatma Gandhi said, "I like your Christ. I do not like your Christians. Your Christians are so unlike your Christ."[24] Friedrich Nietzsche said, "I will believe in the Redeemer when the Christian looks a little more redeemed."[25] Their points are well taken. Only when truth is wrapped in love does it become liberating and empowering. Otherwise it only leads to judgment, arrogance, hatred, and the like.

Maybe truth would be more applauded if those who know it would be nicer about it.

Those of us who are Christ followers must answer for the way we handle truth. It is possible to remain loving while claiming exclusive truth. An immense help to this end would be acknowledging that discovering Christian truth is chiefly a matter of grace—

we only know what we know about God because of his kindness to reveal himself to us. Remember, the only reason we are even open to faith in Jesus to begin with is because we are "taught by God" to come to Jesus.[26] Theologians call it *prevenient grace.* Faith itself is a gift *from* God.[27] Christianity comes *from* God, it works *through* God, and it ends up going back *to* God. The apostle Paul said it best: "For from him and through him and to him are all things. To him be the glory forever!"[28]

It is possible to remain loving while claiming exclusive truth.

This means that truth *knowers* have nothing to boast about. If we want to boast about anything, our only boast can be that God is so good that he actually chased us and caught our imaginations. There is no praise to be assigned to us. All we have going for ourselves is the penchant to run from God. If anything, knowing truth should make us tremble with gratitude as we humbly share with others the treasure we have discovered. There is no room for coercion or *better-than-thou*-ing here.

For the record, however, Christians are not the only ones with a bad history in this regard. Back to Ravi Zacharias, who grew up in India: "Eastern religions have a lot of soul-searching to do in this regard [as well]. Clannish and political conflicts aside, I know of no Christianized country where your life is in danger because you are from another faith. But today there are many countries in the world—such as Pakistan, Saudi Arabia, and Iran—where to become a follower of Christ is to put your life and your family at risk."[29]

>>THE TRUTH STILL HURTS

Because universal truths come across as cutting and untenable in our culture, Christians are often considered irrelevant bigots in the public arena. They tend to respond to this in one of two ways (neither of which is appropriate). Either they get rigid and mean, which makes believers look exclusionary and gated, or they try to fit in by softening their commitment to the truth. They say (only if asked), "I follow Jesus, but everyone has to find his or her own way." This is an attempt to mitigate the sharpness of truth and foster a spirit of harmony between alternative views.

Many Christians have wandered into this fire swamp, holding the position that all truth claims in the domain of faith are just various aspects of the same truth. They suggest that at the end of the day all religions share the same fundamental truths at their core and are only using differing language, divergent stories, and various traditions to communicate those identical beliefs. They assert that the claims of all world religions can be reduced to two basic truths: (a) the universal fatherhood of God, and (b) the universal brotherhood of humankind. As noble as the effort to bring unity is, only those who don't understand the core teachings of world religions would think such a thing possible.

Again, we turn to Ravi Zacharias who says, "What do they mean by the universal fatherhood of God when Buddhism doesn't even claim that there is a God? What do we mean by the fatherhood of God when Shankara, one of the most respected Hindu philosophers, said theism is only a child's way to ultimately get to the top, where you find out God is not distinct from you? What then does the fatherhood of God mean? It is an illusion. This fatherhood of God is not a trans-religious doctrine." After considering the other possible synergies between world religions, Zacharias concludes, "Islam, Buddhism, Hinduism, and Christianity are not saying the same thing. They are distinct and mutually exclusive religious doctrines. They all cannot be true at the same time."[30]

It turns out that the efforts of many to bring unity and encourage respect between people of differing faiths result in nothing more than *syncretism*. Syncretism is the attempt to fuse different belief systems that don't naturally go together—beliefs that are often diametrically opposed to each other. But truth will not "syncretize."

Truth—if one will admit to its reality—is a bit like turning on the light in the middle of the night. It has a stark, unsettling quality to it. Yes, Jesus claims "the truth will set you free";[31] but that's a bit like your doctor saying you'd feel better if you had open-heart surgery. That may be true, but chances are you would avoid an invasive surgery like that unless you believed there was no other way. Truth is just as invasive. It hurts. In surgical-like fashion the writer of Hebrews said truth is "sharper than any double-edged sword, it penetrates even to dividing soul and spirit, joints and marrow; it judges the thoughts and attitudes of the heart."[32] Cutting indeed. This is why embracing something and calling it truth makes you a hero to some and an enemy of others.

Embracing something and calling it truth makes you a hero to some and an enemy of others.

In an attempt to blend the truth claims of world religions, some propose we should adopt the notion that each religion only has a piece of a larger, shared truth—like the ancient fable of the six blind men who examine the elephant. The story goes that the first one touched the elephant's broad, sturdy side and said, "An elephant is like a wall." The second, feeling the round, smooth, sharp tusk said, "No, an elephant is like a spear!" The third happened to take the squirming trunk into his hands and exclaimed, "The elephant is like a snake." The fourth felt around the animal's knee and down to the ground and said, "The elephant is like a tree." The fifth chanced to touch the elephant's ear and announced, "An elephant is like a fan." And the sixth, seizing upon the swinging tail, said with absolute force, "No, an elephant is like a rope." Though they each differed drastically in their descriptions of the elephant, they were all telling the truth. The moral of the story is clear: we may prate on about what we think and about what we believe, and it may sound as if we are telling very different stories; but in the end, believing is the work of the blind—hence, we may all be right.

Nice story and a very, very stimulating philosophical idea. I wish it were true. Here's the problem: the Christian story doesn't fit into the parable. Not only would the Christian hold that Jesus is not like Buddha or Mohammed (who would be seen in the elephant parable as one of the men describing God, who is represented by the elephant), but we hold that Jesus is the elephant. Jesus said to his disciples, "How can you say, 'Show us the Father'?" Then he claimed, "Anyone who has seen me has seen the Father."[33] Jesus isn't the blind prophet teaching about God; Jesus is God incarnate. Scripture claims "the Son is the radiance of God's glory and the exact representation of his being."[34] The truth claim concerning Jesus Christ is far too unique to fit in with any other belief system. So differ-

The truth claim concerning Jesus Christ is far too unique to fit in with any other belief system.

ent is the Christian message that the early followers of Jesus were referred to as atheists because their story could not fit with any other religious story being told in the ancient world. The same holds true today.

Noted theologian N. T. Wright talks about the unique way Jesus Christ portrays God in a world filled with millions of opinions about the matter. In speaking of his work as a college chaplain at Oxford University in England he writes:

> Each year I used to see the first-year undergraduates individually for a few minutes, to welcome them to the college and make a first acquaintance. Most were happy to meet me, but many commented, often with slight embarrassment, "You won't be seeing much of me; you see, I don't believe in God."
>
> I developed a stock response: "Oh, that's interesting. Which god is it you don't believe in?" This used to surprise them. . . . So they would stumble out a few phrases about the god they didn't believe in: a being who lived up in the sky, looking down disapprovingly at the world, occasionally intervening to do miracles, sending bad people to hell while allowing good people to share his heaven. Again, I had a stock response for this very common "spy-in-the-sky" theology: "Well, I'm not surprised you don't believe in that god. I don't believe in that god either."
>
> At this point the undergraduate would look startled. Then, perhaps, a faint look of recognition; it was sometimes rumored that half of the college chaplains at Oxford were atheists. "No,'" I would say, "I believe in the God I see revealed in Jesus of Nazareth."[35]

The Christian doesn't just believe in spirituality or in any description of God. The Christian believes specifically in the God who is revealed in Jesus Christ. He is not just some powerful being who objectifies forces and drives the world. The Christian God is not the god of the pantheists, who is present in everything without personality or passion. Nor is the Christian God the god of the ancient Greeks (Zeus, Hermes, and so on), who is far away and only engages in the affairs of men and beasts when he is angry or after some selfish end. The God revealed in Jesus Christ is personal, the Creator of all that exists, and he is one who longs to care for the human race and for his creation. The Christian God is both other than the world and continually active in it. He is the hope of the world. This is a very different picture from how all other religions portray their gods.

After careful analysis, the Christian is declaring that Jesus Christ is the truest reflection of the one true God, the God of Abraham, Isaac, and Jacob. In the same breath (and at great risk), we are saying that the gods of other religions are not gods at all—they are worthless idols. Ooooo . . . those are fighting words for many. And that's the problem with Christian truth—it is too exclusive to let everything fit. And adhering to it can get you into some deep trouble. That's why Jesus warns us: "The world would love you . . . if you belonged to it; but you don't. I chose you to come out of the world, and so it hates you. Do you remember what I told you? 'A servant is not greater than the master!' Since they persecuted me, naturally they will persecute you."[36]

The Christian is declaring that Jesus Christ is the truest reflection of the one true God.

>>MORE HUMILITY, LESS CONTROL

I believe Christianity is true, but that doesn't mean I think it's okay for me to embrace an us/them dialectic. Nor does it mean that I understand exactly how and when the process of saving faith takes place. I think there is more mystery to the enterprise of faith than most evangelicals allow. But many Christians want to know exactly how and when a person experiences "saving" faith (or the faith that transforms). They want to know, so they can make sure they help get people "there." They're practical. But what if faith isn't as neat and predictable as some Christians think? What if God works in a host of ways in every person's life?

Perhaps those of us who are Christ followers should be less inclined to force everyone into our prefabricated, cookie-cutter salvation framework and be more open to the unique way God may be making himself known in the life of a person. At the very least, these thoughts should make us a little less rabid and biting and a little more interested in the ones we meet—after all, God is already working in their lives before we Christians show up.

This kind of thinking doesn't change the Christian message. It simply changes the sense of control. It causes people to walk into conversations with others, thinking, I wonder what God is doing in your life? instead of, Now that *I* am here, maybe you have a shot at God moving in your life. So much of what evangelicals call evangelism may, in the final analysis, be more hubris than anything else.

What of the idea that God is *already* engaging with folks before they know Jesus? That would mean the job of Jesus followers would be to hunt for the activity of God in the lives of others (that would add some mystery and suspense to faith—like being spies for God!). What if the Christian's job is to help catch God in the lives of others, to point him out, to help make him famous? How fun would that be?

05

>>THE SCIENCE-FAITH SMACKDOWN

it bothers me that science and faith sometimes seem incompatible

Danny DeVito's 1989 movie, *The War of the Roses*, is a sharp and wickedly funny satire that looks at how mean and trivial marital conflict can get. Michael Douglas and Kathleen Turner, along with director DeVito himself, star in the tale where the peaceful life of a married couple, Oliver and Barbara Rose (Douglas and Turner), gets nasty and downright brutal, and the fighting is over the most frivolous issues imaginable. The film depicts how hatred ends up being the stronger where love once was. The story reveals that when people are hurt and feel betrayed, they fight over the smallest and silliest matters.

Historians have recorded another ongoing war of sorts—one between science and faith. It's a kind of science-faith smackdown. But, as is true in many other wars, the fighting doesn't make sense; and in the final analysis, the battles are over issues that are not worth fighting about.

In one corner you have the faith crowd. Why any Christian would have a hard time with science and scientific discovery escapes me. After all, Christians believe that God created the universe, with its laws and peculiarities. Scripture claims, "God's invisible qualities—his eternal power and divine nature—have been clearly seen, being understood from what has been made."[1] Why would we back off from studying and investigating the wonders of the universe? They are snapshots of "God's invisible qualities." We should see science as a pathway to glorify God.

In the other corner you have the scientists. Why any scientist would pick a fight with a person of faith also escapes me. Science is about studying the created, not the Creator. Why would a scientist find belief in a creator threatening? What's the concern? Yet the war rages on.

Science is about studying the created, not the Creator.

Religion is a set of practices and beliefs concerning the cause, nature, and purpose of the universe; science is the effort to study the physical or material world through observation and experimentation. I don't see the need for conflict. Religion doesn't change what scientists do when they do science. If anything, religion has the capacity to do some great things for science: It can raise our imaginative capacities to new heights and motivate us to move beyond our limitations. Science can stimulate our moral sensitivities and focus our concern on the good of others. Belief in God should enrich and animate scientific pursuits. Yet some in the scientific community see religion as an authoritarian imposition that flies in the face of truth. Why? Because throughout history many in the faith community have fought to filter scientific ideas through theological constructs. That really bothers me.

The schism between faith and science is relatively new. As late as the eighteenth century there was a remarkable synergy at play between religion and the sciences. Isaac Newton's (1642–1727) celestial mechanics were widely regarded as completely consistent with the Christian view of God as the Creator of a wonderfully harmonious universe. Members of the Royal Society of London, which was formed to encourage scientific research, were individuals of strong religious conviction who believed that faith enhanced their commitment to scientific discovery and advancement. People saw no conflict between faith and science, at least not until the second half of the nineteenth century. Then things got ugly.

Around 1850, scientists, in knee-jerk response, rejected the criticisms of religious thinkers and began to see themselves as Promethean[2] liberators of humanity, destined to free society from bondage to religious tradition and superstition.

This new paradigm became so prominent in the second half of the nineteenth century that some claimed religion was effectively discredited and in full retreat before a triumphant scientific advance. Over a hundred years ago Thomas Huxley wrote, "Extinguished theologians lie about the cradle of every science as the strangled snakes beside that of Hercules; and history records that wherever science and [faith] have been fairly opposed, the latter has been forced to retire from the lists, bleeding and crushed if not annihilated; scorched if not slain."[3]

>>THE WAY IT BEGAN

The problems started when scientific evidence began to call into question long-accepted viewpoints of those who were authorities in society and culture, many of whom were leaders in the Christian church. Whenever a person discovers a truth that undermines a widely accepted belief, you have fodder for subversive activity. Why? Because the new facts are themselves destructive? Not necessarily. But when new information showed that those in authority didn't have all the answers, those leaders were embarrassed. And if they were wrong about some things—things that were widely accepted—what else were they wrong about? This was when the populace started thinking and asking questions, which potentially undermined the powers-that-be so that those in authority felt threatened. The church's solution? Stop the mess by silencing the ones who asked the questions to begin with—in this case, the scientists.

This problem was exacerbated because religious thought had often homogenized theology into commonly accepted ideas and myths about the world, ideas that have absolutely nothing to do with theology. Remember Copernicus? Back in his day, Copernicus's work contradicted then-accepted religious dogma: the church believed that the sun orbited Earth and that planet Earth was the center of the solar system—and they had the Bible verses to back them up! Some wrote pamphlets protesting Copernicus's new ideas as heresy. Christians believed his work was destroying faith in God. But that was a lie.

Science, almost by definition, is a subversive activity. Scientists must go into a lab with an open mind, without regard to how anyone will respond to what they discover. If they are going to participate in true scientific inquiry, scientists must be willing to stretch beyond what others hold true and dare to think differently.

As science began to make significant advances, the guardians of religion did not like its unbiased approach, so they pushed back. They did not want a change in how things were done. In their view, there was an appropriate way to approach scientific investigation, and that appropriate way ensured that science would never elevate itself above Scripture. But attempting to filter all new ideas through theological constructs felt too restrictive and repressive to the scientists, and by the second half of the nineteenth century the war escalated.

The conflict between science and faith came into full bloom with the appearance of professional scientists and their social struggle to be accepted in nineteenth-century England. At the time, the clergy were the intellectual elites. There were no professional scientists, only individuals who dabbled in scientific inquiry, many of them clergy. The growing conflict had less to do with the differences between science and faith, and more to do with the professional scientists' efforts to displace the clergy and the clergy's fighting back. In order to gain ascendancy in social ranking and influence, the professional scientists portrayed religion in uncomplimentary ways. They were trying to obtain academic freedom from theological restraints as well as the respect and ear of the culture that had not taken them seriously.[4]

Though most would agree that the scientists won (the clergy certainly hold little sway over the popular mind in the twenty-first century), one would be hard-pressed to say science won over faith. The battle never was between the two. Even fairly substantive disagreements turned out to be much more about whether the pope was seen as right (papal politics), whether the church remained in control of the populace (ecclesiastical power struggles), and who got to look like the smart guy (personality/ego issues) than about a fundamental tension between faith and science. Historical scholarship concurs. Oxford scholar Dr. Alister McGrath writes, "The idea that science and religion are in perpetual conflict is no longer taken seriously by any

The problems between science and faith are rooted in social and personal concerns.

major historian of science."[5] The problems between science and faith are not really knowledge or principle based; they are rooted in social and personal concerns.

Today, the war continues as some Christians accuse scientists of being apostate God haters, while some scientists accuse faith advocates of committing intellectual suicide in order to believe in God. Extremists from both camps try to systematically quash each other. Again, careful analysis reveals that the conflict is rooted more in ego and control issues than in anything concrete, which makes me want to yell, "For crying out loud . . . stop it already!"

However, both sides actually do have valid complaints against each other. Let's point out two: honesty about origins and openness to scientific evidence. Scientists need to be more honest when it comes to the debate about the universe's origins, and Christians need to demonstrate more openness in the science-faith conversation. Sadly, it's primarily been Christians who start the fights by getting all nervous about scientific progress.

>>NEED FOR HONESTY IN THE ORIGIN DEBATE

Though the Christian's beliefs are not provable, they are nonetheless perfectly reasonable.

Though no one can prove that God exists, it is reasonable to say that belief is coherent with what we observe in the world. The order and symbiotic nature of the universe *can* be explained by the existence of God as its Creator. But at best, this is a hypothesis, which means another person may hypothesize that the order seen in the world is here by chance. And that hypothesis would not be any less valid than the one offered by the Christ follower.

However, suggesting that a Christ follower is stupid, anti-intellectual, or a science hater because he or she holds to the God hypothesis is not fair. Antifaith attacks are often based on the idea that faith is a childish or infantile notion, like believing in Santa Claus or the tooth fairy. However, beliefs in Santa and the tooth fairy are based on folklore, not evidence. There *is* evidence of God's existence; there are clues. Though some see faith as intellectual nonsense, Christians can stand on the ground that though their beliefs are not provable, they are nonetheless perfectly reasonable—certainly as reasonable as the belief that all things are here by chance.

All evidence can do is show that a belief in God is not inconsistent with what we see in the world.

Evidence That Demands a Verdict

Those who have tried to prove God's existence have had their work mercilessly scrutinized. All attempts end up being surefire recipes for the triumph and expansion of agnosticism and atheism. While there are clues that point to God's existence, clues do not constitute proof. All evidence can do is show that a belief in God is not inconsistent with what we see in the world.

But some of the clues that point to God's existence are more than convincing; they are compelling. *Convincing* means it is likely for something to be true. *Compelling* means a person has to work hard not to end up at the obvious conclusion. There are wagonloads of compelling evidence for the existence of God, but we'll look at just two of the strongest—the ordered universe and the complexities of DNA.

The Truth of Evolution—Micro or Macro?

Let me go off point for just a minute to say that I don't think arguing for God as the Creator of the universe necessitates an attack on the theory of evolution. People on both sides of the fence concede that a form of evolution is taking place all the time. Variations emerge within species of plants and animals—that's why there are so many different kinds of dogs, seedless grapes, hybrid corn, horses that can be bred to race faster, and bacteria that develop immunity to antibiotics. This kind of evolution is referred to as microevolution, and it happens constantly.

But Darwin's theory goes way beyond that, to macroevolution. It claims that, without the guidance of any intelligent designer, life began millions of years ago from a kind of primordial ooze. That ooze gave rise to single-celled creatures, which then evolved into more complex creatures, all the way up to us *homo sapiens*. This is referred to as macroevolution.

Darwin's research challenged the popular Christian notion in the nineteenth century that the world was created in a way that required no modification—the world was perfect. But the Genesis narrative doesn't demand a view of perfection. It simply asserts that God made things to make themselves—this actually implies there was room for modification. In Scripture God speaks to the earth and says, "Let the land produce living creatures according to their kinds: livestock, creatures that move along the ground, and wild animals, each according to its kind."[6] God seems to be saying, "Okay, land, figure out how to bring to fruition what I have started." This could indicate a progression or evolution of some sort. If that is true, it would certainly answer some perplexing questions that science has unearthed, evidenced by fossils records and the presence of vestigial structures. (Vestigial structures are things in a species that seem to have no purpose, like wisdom teeth, the appendix, the tailbone, and the semilunar fold in the corner of the eye.)

Is Darwin's theory true? They definitely have problems, but whether or not macroevolution is true doesn't impact the notion that God is the Creator of the world. Scientific theories about origins simply talk about how things came to be, not whether God was behind it. Even if scientists discover how life emerged, no harm is done to the Christian claim that God was behind its origin. For Christians to argue about scientific theory—*any* theory—because they think it attacks belief in God as Creator seems silly, and that bothers me.

Whether or not macroevolution is true doesn't impact the notion that God is the Creator of the world.

The Truth of the Creation Story—Poetic or Literal?

Let me take this a bit further. What if the point of the creation narrative in Genesis is more poetic than literal? Historically, the church has believed the narrative to be poetic. The church's take was simply that *God created the world.* That's it. Before the nineteenth century, the church never tried to specify how or when God did it. Those in the ancient world (to whom the text was written) did not think in literal or scientific terms, nor would they have cared about such notions. The big news of Genesis to the ancient world was that *one* God, not many, was responsible for all we see. That radical, salient point, which rang through the polytheistic world, had absolutely nothing to do with science.

A belief in God does not necessitate acceptance of the position that the earth is just six thousand years old. The historical, theistic argument is simply that we believe God is the *why* behind what is here, whenever and however it got here. Scientists may ultimately tell us how and when everything happened in ways not articulated in the biblical text, but science will never be able to tell us why. *Why* is the stuff of belief. Understanding this helps Christians be open to the research and questioning of science, while not viewing such questioning as oppositional to faith.

Honestly, I'm not sure where I stand on this matter. In seminary I heard at least seven different theories on how to read the Genesis account—several of them seem very plausible to me. My point here is not to argue for any specific one but simply to say we shouldn't get our undies in a bunch over any of them. The only thing that should matter to the Christian theist is that we believe God created the world—however and whenever it was created. Who cares about the rest? I certainly do not want my kids going to high school or college, believing that the foundation of their faith rests on whether God created the world in six literal days, six thousand years ago!

At the end of the day I think science is actually the friend of faith. Nanoscientist James Tour, a professor at Rice University, spends his life building molecules in the lab. He says, "I stand in awe of God because of what he has done through his creation. Only a rookie who knows nothing about science would say science takes away from faith. If you really study science, it will bring you closer to God."[7] Well said, nanoscience guy.

Now, back to our compelling evidence.

The Evidence of Our Ordered Universe

The universe we live in is amazing. Just the observable universe alone—the universe we know and can talk about intelligibly—is a million million million million (that's 1,000,000,000,000,000,000,000,000) miles across. When we look up into the sky with the naked eye, we can see only about 2000 stars from any given spot on earth. With a pair of binoculars, that number shoots up to 50,000. If you snag a small two-inch telescope, you'd be able to see up to 300,000 stars. With a sixteen-inch telescope you start to count, not stars, but galaxies—up to 100,000 of them, each containing tens of billions of stars. Scientists estimate that there are at least a million different galaxies in just the section of sky framed by the cup of the Big Dipper. And this vastness with all of its complexities works in seemingly perfect order. In describing how the planets work together in our vast solar system, astronomer Geoffrey Marcy remarks, "They're all in the same plane. They're all going around in the same direction. . . . It's perfect, you know. It's gorgeous. It's almost uncanny."[8]

The most compelling evidence—the evidence that seems to scream THERE IS A GOD!—comes from things that are alive.

One could say that the order of nonliving things—the laws that govern physical objects, the earth orbiting the sun, the seasons coming and going, the laws governing atoms and the subatomic universe—is enough evidence to assert that there is a God who designed things to be the way they are. But the most compelling evidence—the evidence that seems to scream THERE IS A GOD!—comes from things that are alive.

The Evidence of DNA

When we turn our attention away from the universe of outer space to the universe of the microscopic, there appears to be as much "inner" space as there is outer space. Even the smallest, single-celled organisms have more complexity within their cellular walls than anything scientists have been able to re-create using huge supercomputers. What guides the process in all living things is the DNA molecule, which regulates every cell of every plant and animal. The DNA molecule is like a tiny microprocessor, and the data encoded on DNA is a kind of written language. The English language uses a twenty-six-letter alphabet; DNA uses a four-letter chemical alphabet. As the chemicals are arranged in various "lettered" sequences, they form what amounts to words, sentences, and paragraphs containing all the instructions needed to guide a living cell. The DNA molecule instructs cells on what and how to eat, how to get rid of waste, when to divide, how to repair themselves, and so on.

The primary role of DNA is the long-term storage of information. Scientists often compare DNA to a set of blueprints, because it contains the instructions needed to manufacture all the internal components of cells, such as proteins and other complex molecules. In addition to regulating everything done on the cellular level, DNA carries all the genetic information (the genes) of an organism. DNA molecules are immensely complex and filled with billions of bits of data. They even know how to replicate themselves when a cell divides so that each new cell has an exact copy of the blueprint to take along with it.

So, where did DNA come from? How was the code "written"? Was it written by chance or was there a Designer?

Dr. Walter L. Bradley, an expert on polymers (a compound that consists of large molecules made of many chemically bonded, smaller, identical molecules) and thermodynamics, says, "Ice crystals have a certain amount of order, but it's simple, repetitive, and has a low amount of information, sort of like filling a book with the words 'I love you, I love you, I love you' over and over again. In contrast, the kind of complexity we see in living matter has a high information content that specifies how to assemble amino acids in the right sequence, like a book being filled with meaningful sentences that communicate a story. Unquestionably, energy can create patterns of simple order. For instance, you could see ripples on the sand at a beach and know they were created by the action of waves. But if you saw the words, 'John loves Mary' and a heart with an arrow drawn in the sand, you know that energy alone didn't create that."[9]

If you and I stumbled onto an ancient drawing on a cave wall or found a novel at an abandoned campsite, we would probably argue that there was intelligence behind it. Doesn't it also seem reasonable that something as complex as the DNA molecule had intelligence behind it? Keep in mind that the DNA molecule is an enormous polymer that contains much more complex information than any cave drawing or novel. It contains the genetic instructions used in the development and functioning of what we call life. Is it really plausible to suggest such complexity happened by chance?

Is it really plausible to suggest such complexity happened by chance?

The 1997 film *Contact* was based on Carl Sagan's novel of the same name. Sagan was an American astronomer and astrochemist who pioneered exobiology and promoted the Search for

Extraterrestrial Intelligence (SETI). In the movie, Dr. Eleanor Arroway, played by Jodie Foster, scans the skies with radio telescopes, searching for signs of intelligent life in space. The radio telescopes are "listening" for a signal that is not the usual static (or white nose), which is the random sound of space. There is no intelligence behind random noise. One day Dr. Arroway begins receiving a signal that is not noise; it is a transmission of prime numbers.

Arroway and the other scientists reason that there is no way a natural cause could be behind a string of numbers like this; it would be too improbable. This was not random static; this was information. It was a message with content. The plot of the film is based on the pursuit to decode and learn from the message that was sent from space. Sagan himself once said, "The receipt of a single message from space would be enough to know there's an intelligence out there."[10]

So here's a valid question: If, as Sagan asserted, a single message from space would be enough for scientists to conclude there is intelligent life out there, what about all the information encoded on the DNA molecule in every living thing? Isn't that evidence that there might be some intelligent Being behind it all? Is it silly to believe an intelligent Designer might be involved?

Suggesting that something as complex as DNA developed without any intelligence directing it is strictly based on the far-fetched odds—more far-fetched than the oft-used analogy of a fully functioning Boeing 747 just showing up after a tornado went through a neighboring junk yard. Could it be that believing life emerged randomly, without an intelligent Designer, actually requires more faith than believing in God?

Again, I am not attacking any scientific theories here, nor am

I trying to blunt our curiosity to discover how things came to be. I'm suggesting that discovering *how* does not preclude the idea that there was intelligence involved. And yet there is much prejudice against this idea in many circles. Case in point: Oxford-educated British chemist Leslie Orgel once said, "Evolution is smarter than you are," to which atheist Christopher Hitchens responded, "But this complement to the 'intelligence' of natural selection is not by any means a concession to the stupid notion of 'intelligent design.'"[11] Why not, Christopher? Why couldn't evolution have an intelligence that was put in it by God? That Hitchens can make no concession to the possibility of God's being involved is evidence of a silly prejudice. It is not a logical observation.

Discovering *how* things came to be does not preclude the idea that there was intelligence involved.

Fat Chance

The odds that everything, both nonliving and living, arrived here by chance would be nearly impossible to calculate. But that doesn't prove things didn't happen by chance; no one can prove that. It does, however, mean that life's arriving by chance is highly, highly, highly improbable (unless the process was rigged by an intelligent Designer).

Let's briefly examine the chances of life's having emerged from some primordial goo without the guidance of an intelligent being. For years scientists worked hard to discover a way to get some simple amino acids to form spontaneously in a soup of organic compounds in the lab. In the 1950s, scientists Stanley Miller and Harold Urey successfully did it. They formed amino acids in a lab container using an atmosphere of methane, ammonia, hydrogen, and an electric spark. Had they found the way life began? Their experiment was initially heralded as a major breakthrough, but problems emerged. Scientists later invalidated their findings because there is no evidence that the earth's atmosphere was ever composed of ammonia, methane, and hydrogen, rather, it is composed of water, carbon dioxide, and nitrogen, which are too inert to react to anything.

Keep in mind that over one hundred amino acids have to be put together in just the right way to make one protein molecule—then it takes about two hundred protein molecules with all the right functions to sustain life in a single cell. Back to Dr. Bradley: "The mathematical odds of assembling a living organism are so astronomical that nobody still believes that random chance accounts for the origin of life. Even if you optimized the conditions, it wouldn't work. If you took all the carbon in the universe and put it on the face of the earth, allowed it to chemically react at the most rapid rate possible, and left it for a billion years, the odds of creating just one functional protein molecule would be one chance in a 10 with 60 zeros after it."[12]

Because of the insurmountable odds for life's emerging spontaneously on earth, new theories are on the rise. Some evolutionary scientists postulate that the building blocks for life must have been deposited here from outer space like seeds or life spores. Even scientists with the caliber of Dr. Francis Crick, the codiscoverer of DNA, have sided with this idea. They suggest that life spores may have been dropped here intentionally by some advanced civilization using Earth as a kind of wilderness area, zoo, or cosmic dump.[13]

I recently heard an interview in which one evolutionary biologist and outspoken antifaith atheist claimed this theory was rich with possibility. It seems odd that one would think it rational to invoke the idea of undetectable spacemen in the name of science, while at the same time arguing that it's insane to even suggest that there might be divine intelligence behind the development of life. According to this gentleman, it would be ridiculous for science to entertain a theological answer but reasonable to consider a science-fiction answer. Hmmm. This is intellectual brilliance?

Both camps practice belief. As far as statistical possibility is concerned, a Creator God seems more tenable than a this-is-all-here-by-chance perspective. But then, I'm biased. I've had an encounter with Jesus Christ.

>>NEED FOR OPENNESS TO SCIENCE

On the flip side, people from all different faith backgrounds have been shamefully reticent about accepting advances in science and have failed to be open to its discoveries. Here are some examples: The Arab mathematician and astronomer Omar Khayyám's work in science was seen as a rebellion against the intellectual constraints of Islam. The work of nineteenth-century Japanese scientists was considered a revolt against the lingering feudalism of their culture. The discipline of twentieth-century Indian physicists ended up being a powerful intellectual counter to the fatalistic ethic of Hinduism. In Western Europe, scientific advance inevitably confronted the culture of the day, including all its political, social, and religious elements. Here the confrontation grew specifically against Christianity.

People from all different faith backgrounds have been shamefully reticent about accepting advances in science.

When it comes to the general advancement of science, Christians have historically hidden behind the Bible and claimed special knowledge whenever new information violated the way they read the Bible. Sadly, Christian folks tend to hunker down into unexamined beliefs—which are often a blend of some good and bad theology—and guard them with a passion. Then they jam these slanted and one-sided views into their understanding of the Christian faith like members of Congress jam their parochial concerns into critical pieces of legislation. Christians are guilty of shoving biases and opinions smack into what they believe the Bible teaches. Here's just one example.

Up until the late 1800s people believed disease was spontaneously generated either by God (or the gods), by devils, or by personal sin. When the idea that disease was instead generated by the reproduction of microorganisms, it was met with strong opposition, especially by those in the church. During the nineteenth century, women in childbirth were dying at alarming rates in Europe and the United States. Up to 25 percent of women who delivered their babies in hospitals died from what was called childbed fever. In the late 1840s, Dr. Ignaz Semmelweis, who worked in the maternity wards of a Vienna hospital, observed that the mortality rate in a delivery room staffed by medical students was up to three times higher than in a delivery room staffed by midwives. In fact, the midwives were terrified of the room staffed by the medical students. Dr. Semmelweis noticed that the students were coming directly from their lessons in the autopsy room to the delivery room. He postulated that they might be carrying the infection from their dissections to birthing mothers. So he ordered doctors and medical students to wash their hands with a chlorinated solution before examining women in labor. This was a completely new idea! When the students followed through, the mortality rate in his maternity wards dropped from 25 percent to less than 1 percent!

Despite the remarkable results, Semmelweis's colleagues greeted his findings with hostility. It was too fantastical. Too ridiculous. Kind of voodooish. (New Agey?) Some believed that trying to fix the mortality problem among mothers and babies was an intrusion on the sovereignty of God. Dr. Semmelweis eventually resigned his position. Later, he had similar dramatic results with hand washing in another maternity clinic, but to no avail. When he died in 1865, his views were still largely ridiculed. Why? Because humans tend to ridicule any new way of looking at things. We fear that embracing a new idea proves we have been wrong (God forbid), and we are too proud for that. This is especially true for those of us in the church.

Humans tend to ridicule any new way of looking at things.

In the midfourteenth century, as the bubonic plague ravaged Europe, there were those who thought it was the judgment of God (just like the TV preachers in the 1980s who claimed AIDS was God's judgment on the homosexuals). But there were others who investigated. Their persistence paid off, and the plague was stopped.

God has created a universe full of laws, presumably to give us ways to participate with him in making this place better. God spoke about the role of the human race in the Genesis narrative, "Let us make man in our image, in our likeness, and let them rule."[14] Can anyone deny that scientific research has led the way for the human race to "rule" over what could have destroyed us?

By appealing too quickly to mystery, people of faith have ended up resistant, intellectually lazy, and passively accepting. Add the concept of radicalized sovereignty (from chapter 3), and you have a whatever-will-be-will-be indolence that shuts out scientific discovery and technological progress.

Christians need to stop being afraid to think outside of the box. They need to be open to reimagining how things work in God's world. They need to quit falling prey to the fearmongers who claim that everything foreign to our current way of thinking must be of the devil.

The church has lost many jewels of the past because those jewels were foreign to church culture. For instance, meditation was widely practiced in the early church, but until recently, modern Christian leaders warned against the practice. The argument against it usually included statements about how people of other faiths—faiths filled with deception—participate in meditation. I have heard preachers say passionately, "Even devil worshippers do it!" But these arguments don't make sense. These folks also eat and sleep. Why don't Christians stop doing those things too? People of other faiths wear clothes and shake each other's hands when they greet each other—are those things wrong too? Turns out that the church has its own version of McCarthyism.

Overreactionary, fear-generating purveyors of woe and danger make their living getting Christians to panic. They are experts at luring folks to come back for more. (No one wants to miss what might hurt them if they don't know about it!) It reminds me of Chicken Little's warning "the sky is falling." Scandalous warnings always yield quite a stir. Fear is contagious. When Chicken Little shared the fear with Henny Penny, Ducky Lucky and Goosey Loosey, you had a really big mess. It turns into a debilitating movement.

So . . . here's my point: just because a scientific idea or theory is new doesn't mean it is wrong. Nor does it mean it's right. Science sometimes gets it wrong. Not long ago science held that the universe was filled with a kind of ether, an inert medium filling up all the space in the universe. Scientists thought this ether was necessary in order for waves of light to travel. So physicists arrived at the theory of the quasirigid, or luminiferous, ether. They were wrong. There was no such thing as ether, and they had to take it out of the textbooks. Science self-corrects as it moves forward in time, which is precisely why people of faith do not need to fall on the sword over issues of science.

We have no idea what is yet to be discovered. I read just today that data from the two space probes NASA launched in 1977, Voyager 1 and Voyager 2, startled astronomers because "the edge of our solar system appears slightly dented as if a giant hand is pushing one edge of it inward."[15] Hmmm. A giant hand? That's the kind of stuff that makes people of faith smile—maybe a God wink? How fun. Christians ought to be excited (and tell their kids to be excited) about what science discovers about how and when—it's interesting stuff.

It takes a tremendous amount of humility to accept that we don't see everything clearly. But we live a lie if we do not unmask the depth of our pretensions, biases, and prejudices and admit that the world's fallenness distorts our reasoning at some level. Seventeenth-century mathematician Blaise Pascal once wrote, "Truly it is an evil to be full of faults, but it is a still greater evil to be unwilling to recognize them."[16] The Scripture says we are fools if we are uncritical about our thinking.[17] Christians must actively pursue outside input and assessment from other people of faith, in addition to the positions taken historically by the church.

>>WHERE FAITH AND SCIENCE DANCE

In the end, we see that there is room for both faith and science. As they each take their places in this world of ours, they come together in a symbiotic dance. It may take some time to sort through new scientific data and locate its congruence within the faith paradigm, but true faith and true science can always live in harmony. After all, God made them both.

Natural science may be able to explain what it observes in the world, but other disciplines are needed to explain why the world is here, what its purpose is, and why order exists. Valid areas of study—like philosophy, sociology, religion, literature, law, and economics—contribute to the observation of phenomena on this planet and hypothesize about it. These areas of study are neither inferior to nor dependent on the natural sciences. They all hold spheres of authority and competency.

Though we can determine much from scientific inquiry, some questions—ones that might be called transcendent—are better off being addressed by religion and metaphysics. Peter Medawar, an Oxford immunologist who won the Nobel Prize in Physiology or Medicine for the discovery of acquired immunological tolerance, wrote, "That there is indeed a limit upon science is made very likely by the existence of questions that science cannot answer, and that no conceivable advance of science would empower it to answer. . . . I have in mind such questions as: How did everything begin? What are we all here for? What is the point of living?"[18]

> Though we can determine much from scientific inquiry, some questions are better off being addressed by religion and metaphysics.

When exploring the unknown, natural scientists depend on

inductive reasoning, which simply means they must weigh evidence and make judgments based on probability, not on proof. Proof is not available, which explains why scientists have so many competing ideas over the same evidence. Any given observation can be explained by a number of theories. When it comes to answering ultimate questions such as the meaning of life or the existence of God, no proof exists. Scientists must concede that such questions cannot be answered or that they have to be answered in another way other than scientifically.

When scientists observe an unexplained phenomenon, they borrow the laws of hypotheses from philosophy as they search for causation. Sometimes their guess is not taken seriously; it's just conjecture to help guide their ongoing investigation (a working hypothesis). These hypotheses are often discarded as new information comes to light or new theoretical interpretations arise. Other times the hypothesis is considered highly probable in the light of all the established facts. Either way, it is all still guesswork, not absolute knowledge.

Discussion about the existence of God are similar. From the vantage point and perspective of reason, both a belief in God and a belief that there is no God are genuine intellectual possibilities as far as science is concerned. The brilliant agnostic Stephen Jay Gould wrote, "Either half my colleagues are enormously stupid, or else the science of Darwinism is fully compatible with conventional religious beliefs—and equally compatible with atheism."[19] The sciences do not move us to a place where there is no conceptual space for God.

Note that Gould's agnostic stance differs from the position of atheists who say believers in God are obscurantists or superstitious reactionaries. Atheists believe science needs to eliminate

God from any place in our understanding of the universe. They hold that atheism is the only tenable answer for the serious, thinking person.

>>WHICH STORY DO YOU BELIEVE?

The Christian's story holds that God is the ultimate source of life, love, and the power behind the universe—no matter what science proves about how it all happened. According to Scripture, the universe is not empty, impersonal space, but a home for God's glory. Scripture teaches that God holds all things together,[20] that his presence "fills the heavens," and that God "stretches out the heavens like a canopy, and spreads them out like a tent to live in."[21] The Christian believes that God's presence is everywhere—on every moon of every world of every star of every galaxy, in every pulsar and quasar and comet and black hole—and he has names for them all. He has a purpose and a plan for everything.

Can you imagine what God sees? He takes in every single sunrise from every possible vantage point. He watches the amazing supernovas and stars that are born as a result. In the Antennae Galaxies alone, which the galaxy astronomers call starburst galaxies, there are hundreds of new star births every year. And God has a front row seat. How cool is that?

In the atheist's story there is no Creator God. The universe is cold, dead, and purposeless; it is the product of random chance, a roll of the dice. In this scenario, things that exist must have always been here; there was no creation event. Matter exists, and that is all that matters. Carl Sagan stated the atheist's theory well, "The Cosmos is all there is, or ever was, or ever will be."[22]

For this crowd, the universe is a closed system. It is not open to being reordered from the outside by any transcendent being. There are no miracles. If there is a god, he or she is irrelevant. Life has no reason, no overarching purpose; it is just what happens, a sequential stream of cause-and-effect events.

According to this view, we are each no one in particular. We are not special or chosen. We arrived here because our lottery number came up. We have no destiny. No one is looking out for us or planning anything for us. Human beings are just complex machines that have personality because of chemical and physical interactions we do not fully understand. Life is not mystery; it is mechanical complexity.

According to this view, we are each no one in particular.

This view holds that death is not a transition from one kind of living to another; it is simply the extinction of personality and individuality. According to the popular twentieth-century philosopher Ernest Nagel, "human destiny [is] an episode between two oblivions."[23] Pretty dark.

In the absence of the Creator, the universe is a giant clock whose gears and levers mesh with mechanical precision, ticking and tocking through time in a perfectly ordered way—all on its own, of course. God is not immanent, not fully personal, and certainly not providential (there is no divine plan).

Which story you hold to be true will profoundly impact the way you feel about yourself and how you respond to the things that happen to you. If this really is a dice-tossed world, life is just a race of the rats, and it's every rat for himself or herself. But if the Bible is true, we matter. It means that what you and I do and how we live counts; we are part of something bigger than ourselves, part of a story God is telling.

Methinks it's a better story.

06

>>AN ALL-TOO-HUMAN CHURCH

it bothers me that so many christians give christianity a bad name

"The church is a whore, but she is my mother."[1] Such was the ranting of one of the early church fathers. For good cause. Why? Because the church frequently loses her way. A cornerstone of Christian theism is the idea that humankind was created to be a reflection of God himself. The Genesis account claims, "God created man in his own image, in the image of God he created him; male and female he created them."[2] Paul says that human beings are to be "imitators of God."[3]

Once God told Moses, "See, I have made you like God to Pharaoh."[4] What if God wants that for each one of us? What if he wants us to be "like God" to others in our walkabout world? That would mean that the way God makes himself known would be primarily through the actions and attitudes of everyday people—men and women, boys and girls, moms and dads, employees and employers, single and married Christ followers.

I'm not saying God doesn't reveal himself directly to people through creation or miracles; he does. But what if God prefers to make himself known through our *humanness*—where our hands become his hands; our words become his words; our care for a child is an extension of his care for that child; our kindness to an injured soul is a reflection of his?

Jesus alluded to this when he told his disciples, "Anyone who has seen me has seen the Father."[5] He says something strikingly similar about those who follow him: "I tell you the truth, anyone who has faith in me will do what I have been doing."[6] And then again in prayer to the Father, "As you sent me into the world, I have sent them into the world."[7] The imagery is clear: when someone asks, "Where is God?" Christ followers should be able to respond, "You're looking at him."

I'm not suggesting that Christian people are God. I am simply pointing out that God wants Christians to be (as Jesus was) a reflection of God, to be his image bearers. People of faith need to live in such a way that they can say, "If you watch me, you will see Jesus." This is the heart of why Christians are called the body of Christ. If you want to know where Ed Gungor is right now, locate my body. If people want to find God, find his image bearers.

Sadly, that has not been the case. History is chock full of examples of people doing evil and injustice in the name of God—Christ followers included. Eugene Peterson writes, "Religion is the most dangerous energy source known to humankind. The moment a person (or government or religion or organization) is convinced that God is either ordering or sanctioning a cause or a project, anything goes. The history, worldwide, of religion-fueled hate, killing, and oppression is staggering."[8]

That some Christians would harm others in the name of Christ is puzzling. The life and claims of Jesus Christ had absolutely nothing to do with injustice, violence, and coercion. What's up with his followers? The disconnect between Christ and his followers has given Christianity a bad name. Many have blown off Christianity because of the evils done by Christians. One critic vented, "Christianity has (by some people) been used throughout history as an excuse for some of the most brutal, heartless, and senseless atrocities known to man. Historical examples are not difficult to recall: the Crusades; the Inquisitions; the witch-burnings; the Holocaust. . . . I did not see much in Christianity that I considered to be worth the having."[9]

No question about it: some Christians have acted badly, very badly. Christ followers have to own that much harm has been done in the name of Jesus Christ by some who claim to be his followers. It is hard to imagine, but Christians have been purveyors of coercion, pain, horror, and death in their quest to establish God's kingdom in the world. They have been guilty of violence against racial minorities, women, Jews, abortionists, homosexuals, and people of other faiths. Somehow Christians have transformed Jesus' message of loving others and turning the other cheek into a doctrine of murder and force. The cheap, short answer as to why would be to claim that those who participated in these atrocities were not true followers of Jesus. In some cases that would be true. Jesus himself warned, "Not everyone who says to me, 'Lord, Lord,' will enter the kingdom of heaven, but only he who does the will of my Father who is in heaven. Many will say to me on that day, 'Lord, Lord, did we not prophesy in your name, and in your name drive out demons and perform many miracles?' Then I will tell them plainly, 'I never knew you. Away from me, you evildoers!'"[10]

> No question about it: some Christians have acted badly, very badly.

Suggesting, however, that everyone who has participated in

the evils done by the church was a false follower Jesus spoke of would be a convenient escape hatch. We don't want to admit how easily Jesus' nonviolent, respect-all-people position has been abandoned in favor of coercion and force—especially when the goal has been to advance the kingdom of God. Power is seductive indeed, especially when one's cause is perceived as an eternal mandate from God Almighty.

Let's explore a few connective tendrils of thought that have allowed the church to justify actions that were clearly in opposition to the teachings of Christ.

>>THE WAY WE WERE

Christianity began with a small group of Christ followers in the backwaters of the Roman Empire. In its first stage, it wasn't a religion. It was a grassroots movement of people gathering around the person of Jesus Christ and living a certain way—in fact, Christianity was referred to as the Way.[11] Early Christians did not value buildings, hierarchy, or political clout, nor did they curry favor with the state. Instead, they sought to live differently, to live prophetically, as a critique to the misplaced values and beliefs of the cultures surrounding them.

Those early Christians would have considered it idolatry to run after earthly power.

The early church had little money, no mass-media budget, no political power, and little ecclesiastical structure and authority. The movement depended on the simplicity and effectiveness of a one-on-one, person-to-person influence. There was no thought of expanding God's kingdom through force or manipulation. Those early Christians would have considered it idolatry to run after earthly power (political or otherwise). They believed God expanded his kingdom through his Son, Jesus Christ, and through the lifestyle of the church, Christ's body.

Having little wealth or political power was not considered weak or insignificant. These Christians knew God's kingdom would grow in the midst of big evil—Roman evil. They expected the kingdom to spread like a flu virus from one person to another until it reached the whole world. And grow it did!

Historians have long marveled at the speed with which Christianity spread throughout the Roman Empire, despite intense persecution. Atheist-turned-Christian Patrick Glynn observes, "Part of the reason for Christianity's rapid spread, historians have remarked, was simply that the early Christians were such nice people. The kindness of the Christians and their service to the poor and downtrodden attracted new adherents. 'Christians astounded the ancients with their charity,' as one historian put it."[12]

Part of the reason for Christianity's rapid spread was simply that the early Christians were such nice people.

These early Christians were not just known for taking care of their own, but also for caring for their neighbors, those who were poor, sick, or otherwise hurting. This surprised those outside the movement. Even the skeptics gave Christians backhanded compliments. Lucian, a second-century satirist and critic of Christianity wrote:

> These misguided creatures start with the general conviction that they are immortal for all time, which explains the contempt of death and voluntary self-devotion which are

> so common among them; and then it was impressed on them by their original lawgiver that they are all brothers, from the moment that they are converted, and they deny the gods of Greece, and worship the crucified sage, and live after his laws. All this they take quite on faith, with the result that they despise all worldly goods alike, regarding them merely as common property.[13]

These early Christians had a fearless devotion to the faith (they were willing to lay down their lives for it), but they also were humble and compassionate to others, even to those who rejected them and caused them harm. Their undying care for one another, along with their commitment to the disenfranchised poor and needy in their communities, caused their influence in the ancient world to be profound.

Bad Moon Rising

By the third century, the early church had cultivated a full-blown expression of faith called Christianity, with its own sacred books, its own rituals, and its own ideas. This was also a time of great confrontation with the Roman Empire. This burgeoning new religion, from Rome's perspective, was threatening the social order and ultimately the political order of the Empire. And just as all bureaucracies do, the Roman Empire tried to protect itself, to perpetuate itself by fighting the threat. But the Romans failed to beat down Christianity through persecuting its adherents. In fact, by the fourth century Christianity actually became the state religion, by the end of *that* century, it was illegal throughout the entire Roman Empire to participate in any form of public worship other than Christianity. How did that happen?

The surprising twist came through the emperor Constantine. Constantine was a successful general who claimed to have had a vision that called him to fight in Christ's name, so he became a Christian. Technically, Constantine was not so much a convert to Christianity as he was a patron of the faith, and the benefits of the imperial patronage he bestowed on the Christian church were enormous. He legitimized Christianity as the protected religion of the empire and lavishly supported it with both political and economic power.

The bishops were grateful for the imperial attention and formed a symbiotic relationship with the empire (instead of being hunted and killed by it). For centuries, church and civic authorities worked together holding the seat of power and control over society. Imperial ideology and Christian tradition were merged. The result was that the church no longer thought of Jesus as the Jewish suffering servant who claimed, "My kingdom is not of this world"[14] Through his church, the Kingdom of Rome was now in Jesus' hands. Roman statues of Jesus began to depict him as an emperor. He became the imperial Jesus enthroned as part of the mainstream of Roman society.

This marriage between the church and the state became a terrible thing.

But this created problems. While it was wonderful that the merciless persecution of Christians stopped, Constantine's extravagant favor on the church opened the door for it to become too closely aligned with the state and its powers. Church leaders believed God was providentially handing them access to political and financial power, including access to the sword, if need be. The church now had clout and money and the strong arm of the state to force the kingdom of God on the earth. Christians thought this was surely the hand of God working in history. They believed the kingdom of heaven had come to earth. But this marriage between the church and the state became a terrible thing.

Up until then, the Christian church had never tasted secular power. Turns out that influencing others is much more complex and time consuming than forcing them to do what you want. And when you believe it's up to *you* to defend God's honor and save the world, it's easy to justify grabbing whatever powers you have at your disposal to force compliance. And that's what those fourth-century Christian leaders did. The political clout and financial strength was too seductive to resist.

Soon after the church was bequeathed with the powers of the state, it began to use force in various church-oriented activities. For example, missionary expansion started being done in heavy-handed fashion.

The Holy Roman Emperor Charles the Great gave an imperial decree to the Saxons which declared, "If there is anyone of the Saxon people lurking among them unbaptized, and if he scorns to come to baptism and wishes to be absent himself and stay pagan, let him die."[15]

Forced Purity

Then there was the issue of doctrinal and ethical purity. Early on, church leaders confronted error through instruction and encouragement, while keeping love, respect, and relationship the top priority. Things changed around the time the church gained political and financial strength. St. Augustine, a witness to this newfound power, reasoned that if torture was appropriate for the state to use against those who broke the laws of men, it was even more fitting for those who broke the laws of God.[16]

During the dark centuries that followed, Christian leaders began to justify using torture to keep heretics from gaining influence in the church. A heretic was anyone who held a theological or religious opinion or doctrine that was contrary to the orthodox doctrine of Christianity. This was extended to include opinions about philosophy, politics, science, art, and the like. The leaders believed they had authority over all church members in such matters. And instead of love and brotherhood being the primary issue, being right and touting the party line were held sacrosanct. This new breed of leaders felt it was appropriate to use force to shut the mouths of those who disagreed with them. Without regret, they used iron collars with spikes to impale the throats of those who opposed them doctrinally as well as stretching machines that tore people apart. All in the name of God, of course.

Their sick reasoning is captured in St. Dominic's discourse against one particular group of so-called heretics who held a different philosophical view than the church had espoused. Dominic wrote, "For many years I have exhorted you in vain, with gentleness, preaching, praying, weeping. But according to the proverb of my country, 'where blessing can accomplish nothing, blows may avail.' We shall rouse against you princes and prelates, who, alas, will arm nations and kingdoms against this land."[17]

Scores of popes, bishops, friars, and priests attacked so-called heresy in earnest. They eventually added the rule that all property belonging to a convicted heretic would be forfeited to the church, then shared with local officials and the victim's accusers. This became a great motivation to find more and more heretics.

Here's another story that shows how cavalier and uncontested the heretical purge process became:

> In 1234, the canonization of Saint Dominic was finally proclaimed in Toulouse, and Bishop Raymond de Fauga was washing his hands in preparation for dinner when he heard the rumor that a fever-ridden old woman in a nearby house was about to undergo the Cathar ritual. The bishop hurried to her bedside and managed to convince her that he was a friend, then interrogated her on her beliefs, then denounced her as a heretic. He called on her to recant. She refused. The bishop thereupon had her bed carried out into a field, and there she was burned. "And after the bishop and the friars and their companions had seen the business completed," Brother Guillaume wrote, "they returned to the refectory and, giving thanks to God and the Blessed Dominic, ate with rejoicing what had been prepared for them."[18]

We could go on to the horror of the Crusades—so much cruel and needless bloodshed. We could cite the destruction of thousands through the Dark Ages who were guilty of little more than being ugly, old, widowed, or mentally ill yet were convicted of crimes that would have been impossible for them to commit and then murdered for God's sake. Here's one anecdote typical of what would happen:

> In 1595, an old woman residing in a village near Constance, angry at not being invited to share the sports of the country people on a day of public rejoicing, was heard to mutter something to herself, and was afterwards seen to proceed through the fields towards a hill, where she was lost sight of. A violent thunderstorm arose about two hours afterwards, which wet the dancers to the skin, and did considerable damage to the plantations. This woman, suspected before of witchcraft, was seized and imprisoned, and accused of having raised the storm, by filling a hole with wine, and stirring it about with a stick. She was tortured till she confessed, and burned alive the next evening.[19]

Somehow these Christian leaders forgot the Jesus of the New Testament, who surely wept in horror and sadness at the atrocities done in his name. Jesus' way was to heal the sick and challenge accusers to cast the first stone only if they themselves were sinless.

It bothers me that doctrinal and ethical purity are seen as more important than love, respect, and relationship.

Worldly powers, whether political, social, or financial, blinded the saints. The premise that power corrupts certainly proved true during this time.

This thinking has dominated religious thought right up to the present day. While Christian leaders no longer use iron collars with spikes, they use whatever power is at their disposal—emotional, political, economic, and psychological—to quell perceived heresy and keep the flock under their control.

>>POWER VS. INFLUENCE

Certainly God wants his kingdom established in this world, but he has never been interested in getting it done through broken human systems. God knows that, like the ring worn by Bilbo in Tolkien's Lord of the Rings trilogy, secular power corrupts the soul.

Scripture tells us that "the devil took [Jesus] to a very high mountain and showed him all the kingdoms of the world and their splendor. 'All this I will give you,' he said, 'if you will bow down and worship me.'"[20] Jesus was not into kingdoms or splendor, at least not the kind found here. His followers tried to force him to rebel against Rome and declare himself king; they figured he had the supernatural powers to pull it off.[21] But he refused. In truth, God sees the political, economic, military, and social powers of this world (and their ilk) as worthless: "Surely the nations are like a drop in a bucket; they are regarded as dust on the scales. . . . Before him all the nations are as nothing; they are regarded by him as worthless and less than nothing."[22]

Christendom is about power; Christianity is about influence.

Yet, in spite of Jesus' teaching, the church amassed earthly power and took on a public identity that was smug, arrogant, triumphalist, uncompassionate, and morally superior. Simple Christianity was overtaken by a kingdom Christianity, referred to as Christendom. Christendom is about power; Christianity is about influence.

Power attempts to change others, but influence begins humbly with one's self. The Christian realizes that he or she, most of all, needs to change within and be conformed to the image of Christ.

Power tempts us to believe we need to convince, coerce, or overpower others. Power also leads us to be argumentative, judgmental, and confrontational, which ironically doesn't change anyone. Influence, in contrast, leads us to be kind, forgiving, and loving. True Christianity does not purport to claim that changing others is a human responsibility. The Christian's job is to faithfully be a witness to God's presence and love. God does the changing.

My wife, Gail, and I are parents of four adult children. We used to have power over them; now we have no real power, but we do have plenty of influence. Truth be told, we prefer to influence rather than enforce. Influence lends itself more to respect for and faith in our kids and is less centered on us being superior. We like nurturing and supporting more than bossing and ruling.

Not long before her death, Mother Teresa spoke at one of the most prestigious Ivy League schools in the Northeast. Prior to her visit, previous Christian speakers had been welcomed to campus with protests, catcalls, and disruptions during their speeches. So I was surprised and delighted to hear how warmly and respectfully the audience received Mother Teresa. I think the reason is because she was a symbol of powerlessness. When she spoke, she wasn't after political, intellectual, or social currency; she simply told her story and asked the audience to consider the desire of Christ to protect life and care for the hurting and dying. During the ninety-minute speech the room was silent, and she received a standing ovation at the end.

Power doesn't always win in the end—there may be someone else who is more powerful than you—but influence always wins. Whenever the church has strayed from influence to power, she has become corrupt and cruel. Those who want to return to the spirit of true Christianity must give up the lust for power.

Antipower

When Christians feel the weight of the world on their shoulders, they lash out at anyone they believe opposes God's ways. If Christians do not want to fail in the future, they must learn from history. The kingdom of God is not about the use of power. It's about the hope of influence, which is a kind of *anti*power. When power is the strategy and battle plan, the goal becomes forcing opponents to think "like I do." Power relies on force, leverage, superior numbers, maneuvering. It's about vanquishing the enemy, utterly annihilating the opponent. No mutual respect and bridge-building here.

Jesus introduced the idea of changing the world through *anti*power. Whenever one of his followers tried to push him into a position of power, he refused to go there. At one point in his ministry the crowd "intended to come and make [Jesus] king by force, [so he] withdrew again to a mountain by himself."[23] Another time, Peter grabbed a sword and used it in an attempt to protect Jesus.[24] Jesus told him that violence was not appropriate for advancing the kingdom. Still another time, two of Jesus' disciples tried to use violence to teach some Christ rejecters a lesson.[25] Again, Jesus turned and rebuked them. He was aware that human-controlled religion gets violent and corrupt very quickly. He consistently referenced how the religious professionals of his day were crooked and dangerous. He warned his followers not to default to doing things the way they did.[26]

Christ followers are to imitate this sacrificial gesture. "To this you were called," Scripture says, "because Christ suffered for you, leaving you an example, that you should follow in his steps."[27] This is how we make room for God's kingdom to change people and ultimately the world.

The teachings of sacrifice, kindness, forgiveness, humility, and love are unavoidable, inescapable themes of the Bible.

When Power Backfires

Many Christians have developed amnesia when it comes to applying these truths to daily life. Those who ignore Christ's teachings (and history) try to redeem the culture through duress, using things like political activism and partisan politics. But this warfare mind-set always backfires.

Many forget that they, too, were once enemies of God.[28] Instead of empathy, they feel superior toward those who reject God. They see themselves as the only true friends God has and become self-appointed border guards of the kingdom. In unimaginative, hackneyed form, they ape first-century citizens and try to make Jesus king by force, unwittingly discrediting God's name. Accordingly, Christians lose influence.

Power might promise control and votes, but it does not win hearts and minds.

This is what happened when the doors of the Oval Office were thrown open to evangelical Christians in the 1980s, and presidential candidates sought the votes of Christians. The access to the corridors of power was a heady brew. Suddenly, conservative Christians had a voice in the political arena and began to see power as the best way to spread biblical values, enforce moral standards, and eventually prevail in the culture wars. Unfortunately, as Christians chose to leverage this newfound power, they lost influence. Power might promise control and votes, but it does not deliver influence. It does not win hearts and minds.

Influence Is Never Safe

Influence is never safe, and it's not flashy or popular. Influence is found on a narrow, straight, and hard road that seems to violate common sense. It requires self-sacrifice, humility, altruism, and reckless love. Influence is being the good Samaritan.[29] Influence is binding up your enemy's wounds and caring for him at your own expense.

I love what Erwin McManus says in this regard: "Somehow we all know that to play it safe is to lose the game."[30] Influence requires involvement and engagement, while power wages war from a safe distance. Siding with influence requires us to find the balance between redeeming culture and remaining separate from the world. It's risky and won't bring personal glory. But it *will* win the heart of our neighbors.

>>FOLLOWING JESUS

To follow Christ is a call to surrender in the culture war. This means ditching the power weapons. It means refusing to leverage political alliances, demonize the opposition, and form pressure groups that use pressure tactics.

Instead of power, Jesus followers must choose influence. They must adopt the *anti*power initiative modeled by Jesus Christ and die for those who need transformation. Christians do this by reacting to evil with good and responding to hatred with love and kindness. Antipower takes shape when Christians go the extra mile and turn the other cheek; when they pray for their enemies and make peace with those who oppose them.

When Christians follow Jesus' example of authentic sacrifice, they stop investing their energies in defending or advancing their own religion, ideologies, or tribe. Rather, they love as God loves—without reservation or condition. They no longer live in an "eye for eye" or "tooth for tooth" world; they don't return evil for evil or hatred for hatred. Instead, they give a blessing. True Christianity—Christianity that is not bothersome—drops the us-versus-them frame of mind. Labels disappear, and people are seen only as individuals for whom Christ died.

Is this hard? You bet. So hard it may kill you. But isn't that what it means to take up one's cross to follow Jesus? From its inception Christianity has always involved death on some level. Why should it be any different today?

Jesus overcame evil in this world and changed people's lives by sacrificing himself for them. He didn't war against people to change them. Nor did he enact change by starting a political organization or rounding up votes for Election Day or badmouthing sin. There was nothing forceful about Jesus. He didn't come to earth to conquer us. Instead, he came in weakness. He came to die. This is not Patton or MacArthur, Rambo or Iron Man. This is Jesus. He is the ultimate example of what it looks like to win by losing. Only God would promote something so preposterous.

When Christians dare to live as Christ did, they will reflect the teachings of Christ and restore his good name.

07

>>AN OLD TESTAMENT "BULLY"

it bothers me that God looks like such a bully in the old testament

In 1794, Thomas Paine wrote, "Whenever we read the obscene stories, the voluptuous debaucheries, the cruel and torturous executions, the unrelenting vindictiveness, with which more than half the Bible is filled, it would be more consistent that we called it the work of a demon, than the word of God."[1]

Even a casual reading of the Old Testament leaves one wondering how a loving God could order the execution of every firstborn Egyptian child; flood the known world, killing untold thousands of people; order the extermination of entire nations—including women and children; and demand the sacrifice of innocent animals as a way of making up for human failure. *Who is this God?* Thomas Jefferson was known to say that the Old Testament reveals God to be "cruel, vindictive, capricious and unjust."[2]

From a casual view, the New Testament's description of Jesus Christ appears incongruent with the Old Testament description of the God of the Jews. The starkness of the disparity caused some early church fathers to argue that the God of the Old Testament could not have been the Father Jesus referred to in his teachings.

Though that notion did not become the orthodox view, the problem remained. If we claim that the God of the Old Testament is the Christian God, how can we say that God is good and morally pure in light of all the recorded atrocities? How do we make sense of it?

There are no easy answers, but here is a provocative view, a "maybe" that seems tenable.

>>BEFORE THE CROSS

God, since the great Fall of humankind, has been engaged in a battle against evil. He hates evil and has always been bent on destroying it. To that end, Moses identified God early on as a being "of war."[3] From the moment sin spilled into the world, God enacted a strategy to fight evil and rescue us from its control.

Before the cross God fought evil toe-to-toe in the boxing ring of the physical world. To hold back evil, he had to physically destroy the people who were perpetrating it. The person and the evil were destroyed together. For example, Scripture asserts that just prior to the flood only one family was even open to God. "The Lord saw how great man's wickedness on the earth had become, and that every inclination of the thoughts of his heart was only evil all the time."[4] To stop the death of faith and to halt evil from totally pervading the human race, God sent a great flood. This action was necessary to save the human race, though it grieved God's heart.[5]

Examples abound of God destroying evil by destroying people. False prophets, who lied about speaking for God, were to be executed: "But a prophet who presumes to speak in my name anything I have not commanded him to say, or a prophet who speaks in the name of other gods, must be put to death."[6] Adulterers received capital punishment: "If a man commits adultery . . . both the adulterer and the adulteress must be put to death."[7] Some sins were so evil that even if a child committed them, the child (and the sin) met with death: "Anyone who attacks his father or his mother must be put to death. . . . Anyone who curses his father or mother must be put to death."[8] (I'm not sure many of us from the West would have made it through adolescence if those commands were still in play.) If you harmed your neighbor, you were to be injured as retribution: "If anyone injures his neighbor, whatever he has done must be done to him: fracture for fracture, eye for eye, tooth for tooth. As he has injured the other, so he is to be injured."[9]

Numerous places in Scripture say God killed people[10] or ordered them to be killed. He commanded Israel to be a warring people: "When the LORD your God brings you into the land you are entering to possess and drives out before you many nations . . . you must destroy them totally. Make no treaty with them, and show them no mercy."[11] Israel was not to lie down and let wicked nations overrun her.

Because he was holy and committed to the world and the people he created, he squashed evil.

Commands such as these create confusion. Scripture also claims "God is love,"[12] and it's difficult to reconcile wrath with love. The truth is, the God of the Old Testament did love people. God always has. Nothing in him wants to destroy people. But because he was holy and committed to the world and the people he created, he squashed evil. The problem was if a person clung to the evil God planned to destroy, that person (or group) got destroyed too.

>>CAVEATS TO KEEP IN MIND

When reading the violent history of the Old Testament, remember that what happened was not necessarily what God *wanted* to happen. God did numerous things that he did not want to do. For example, in Ezekiel God warned of an impending judgment that was coming to Israel:

> The people of the land practice extortion and commit robbery; they oppress the poor and needy and mistreat the alien, denying them justice. . . . So I will pour out my wrath on them and consume them with my fiery anger, bringing down on their own heads all they have done, declares the Sovereign LORD.[13]

This text is similar to the many others expressing how God wrestled with idolatrous Israel, warning her, calling out to her, warning her again, and then promising to bring destruction in order to bring her evil ways to a halt. This particular text offers us a rare Old Testament glimpse into the heart of God behind his role as judge. Sandwiched in between the harsh tone of the two verses above is one that shows us that God really does have a soft heart and is more like a father than judge:

> I looked for a man among them who would build up the wall and stand before me in the gap on behalf of the land so I would not have to destroy it, but I found none.[14]

God was looking for a way out. He does not delight in doling out judgment any more than any earthly parents enjoy doing so to their children. A careful study of Scripture reveals that God doesn't commit to judgment unless absolutely necessary—until he has exhausted every other possibility. Turns out that God is not "cruel, vindictive, capricious, or unjust" after all.

God doesn't commit to judgment until he has exhausted every possibility.

Story after story in the sacred text shows God waiting for humans to intervene and stop the negative action that he, as Judge, was being painted into a corner to make. Here are just a few: Once Moses and God were on Mount Sinai, and God, after vowing to wipe his idolatrous people out, waited and allowed Moses to talk him out of it.[15] After God told Abraham his plan for destroying Sodom and Gomorrah, he let Abraham negotiate with him. Abraham convinced God to halt the plan as long as the angels could find ten righteous people.[16] However, there were not even ten. There's also the story of righteous Hezekiah who pleaded for his life in the face of God's seemingly inalterable decree of judgment. As Hezekiah prayed, God added another fifteen years to his life.[17]

Throughout the Old Testament, God is described as merciful. The word translated "mercy" is found in the Bible 261 times—and a full two thirds of them are found in the Old Testament! The word *love* is found over three hundred times (about half in each of the Testaments). The point is, God's character of love and mercy is revealed in *both* Testaments. It's just harder to see these qualities in the Old Testament. But don't be mistaken. Though it may not be immediately obvious to the casual onlooker, God's heart is merciful. The ancient Israelites knew this. They saw God as notoriously merciful. We know this because of responses like the one from the prophet Jonah.

>>THE BELLY DANCE

Remember Jonah . . . the in-the-belly-of-the-fish guy? The story goes, "One day long ago, God's Word came to Jonah, Amittai's son: 'Up on your feet and on your way to the big city of Nineveh! Preach to them. They're in a bad way and I can't ignore it any longer.' But Jonah got up and went the other direction to Tarshish, running away from God."[18] Jonah didn't *want* the Ninevites to repent. (The Israelites hated the Ninevites.) He knew that if they repented, God might spare them. Jonah ran from God and ended up as fish bait.

But after becoming fish vomit, Jonah decided he had no choice but to preach to the citizens at Nineveh: "Jonah entered the city, went one day's walk and preached, 'In forty days Nineveh will be smashed.'" But the Ninevites did the unexpected: "The people of Nineveh listened, and trusted God. They proclaimed a citywide fast and dressed in burlap to show their repentance. Everyone did it—rich and poor, famous and obscure, leaders and followers."[19] Their repentance went all the way to their top leaders: "When the message reached the king of Nineveh, he got up off his throne, threw down his royal robes, dressed in burlap, and sat down in the dirt. Then he issued a public proclamation throughout Nineveh, authorized by him and his leaders: 'Not one drop of water, not one bite of food for man, woman, or animal, including your herds and flocks! Dress them all, both people and animals, in burlap, and send up a cry for help to God. Everyone must turn around, turn back from an evil life and the violent ways that stain their hands. Who knows? Maybe God will turn around and change his mind about us, quit being angry with us and let us live!'"[20]

To Jonah's horror, God forgave them: "God saw what they

had done, that they had turned away from their evil lives. He did change his mind about them. What he said he would do to them he didn't do."[21] By this point Jonah was majorly hacked off at God:

> Jonah was furious. He lost his temper. He yelled at God, "God! I knew it—when I was back home, I knew this was going to happen! That's why I ran off to Tarshish! I knew you were sheer grace and mercy, not easily angered, rich in love, and ready at the drop of a hat to turn your plans of punishment into a program of forgiveness! So, God, if you won't kill them, kill me! I'm better off dead!"
>
> God said, "What do you have to be angry about?" But Jonah just left. He went out of the city to the east and sat down in a sulk.[22]

Again, a careful exegesis of the Old Testament reveals that God is soft at heart. An image from the 1939 film *The Wizard of Oz* comes to mind. The Wizard, played by actor Frank Morgan, turns out to be a kind, fatherly man who appeared rather scary early on—with a big projected video head and a loud, booming voice. One could surmise that the wizard was being deceptive; but I take it that his tactics were necessary. After all, he had to hold the attention of the citizens of Emerald City who were constantly being threatened by witches and flying monkeys. They probably didn't feel as safe with "kind" as they did with "powerful."

Perhaps the reason God comes across so big and mean in many of the Old Testament texts is because he needed to be like that in order for the Israelites to feel safe and protected. The ancient world was filled with wagonloads of violence and hardship, which made people hard and calloused. Hard-hearted folks tend to respond much better to power than they do to kindness and mercy (at least in the short haul).

This is the rub in a fallen world. People get beat up and hurt, which leads to an internal hardness about life. And people with hard hearts act selfishly and often unpredictably. Dealing with people like this demands employing rules that are more brutal than one would like, for instance when a government imposes martial law during wars or occupations because civil order has fallen apart.

Another example of how God accommodates the hardhearted is found in Jesus' teaching on divorce. The men of his day asked him what his take was on the subject. Jesus said divorce shouldn't happen, period. They were flabbergasted: "They shot back in rebuttal, 'If that's so, why did Moses give instructions for divorce papers and divorce procedures?' Jesus said, 'Moses provided for divorce as a concession to your hardheartedness, but it is not part of God's original plan.'"[23]

Think of that. Concessions were made because of their "hardheartedness." God hates divorce,[24] but he allowed it because people's hearts were not open to his higher standard for the home.

Much of how God functioned in the Old Testament was because people's hearts were desperately hard. Judgment was never God's highest dream. It did not represent his loving heart. It was a "concession," a desperate one. The Latin phrase *extremis malis extrema remedia*, loosely translated, is "Desperate times call for desperate measures." Perhaps this is the why behind God's turbulent actions in the pre-Jesus world.

Dealing with people like this demands employing rules that are more brutal than one would like.

When you see these things, you find yourself giddy in the understanding that there is only one God in the Old and New Testament and he is not two-faced or schizophrenic. Even in his times of Old Testament judgment, God always has been and always will be a God of love.

Much of how God functioned in the Old Testament was because people's hearts were desperately hard.

But under the new covenant, everything changed. The work of Christ made a way to change and soften the human heart.

>>HERE COMES JESUS

Though the identical, unchangeable God is in both Testaments, his love is not as clearly seen in the Old as in the New. The writer of Hebrews pens,

> In many separate revelations [each of which set forth a portion of the Truth] and in different ways God spoke of old to [our] forefathers in and by the prophets.[25]

This means the ancient Jews saw God's nature and essence in the Old Testament in bits and pieces—not perfectly or completely. Then the writer continues:

> [But] in the last of these days He has spoken to us in [the person of a] Son. . . . He is the sole expression of the glory of God [the Light-being, the out-raying or radiance of the divine], and He is the perfect imprint and very image of [God's] nature.[26]

It's only when Jesus comes into view that we see God clearly! Jesus is the "perfect imprint" and the "very image" of God's nature. In Jesus we see who God is and how he really wants to handle things. We see that he longs to address the wrongs in the world through kindness and grace, not violence. Jesus is not a bit or a piece of revelation about God; he is God *enfleshed*. Earlier we saw that Jesus declared about himself, "Anyone who has seen me has seen the Father."[27] If you want to see what God actually looks like, look at Jesus.

In Jesus, God deals with evil on a *spiritual* plane, not just on the physical side of the equation.

Something new was put in motion when Jesus arrived on the scene. Jesus brought God's higher law and purpose for humanity to the fore. Remember, God's Old Testament laws ordered retribution on a *person* who was responsible for acting in an evil way. "If anyone injures his neighbor, whatever he has done must be done to him: fracture for fracture, eye for eye, tooth for tooth. As he has injured the other, so he is to be injured."[28]

But when Jesus came, he shocked everyone:

> You have heard that it was said, "Eye for eye, and tooth for tooth." But I tell you, do not resist an evil person. If someone strikes you on the right cheek, turn to him the other also. And if someone wants to sue you and take your tunic, let him have your cloak as well. If someone forces you to go one mile, go with him two miles. Give to the one who asks you, and do not turn away from the one who wants to borrow from you. You have heard that it was said, "Love your neighbor and hate your enemy." But I tell you: Love your enemies and pray for those who

> persecute you, that you may be sons of your Father in heaven."[29]

Jesus introduced the radical idea of *not* demanding retribution from the one who caused evil. He revealed that this is God's highest way—the path God would have always preferred to use in addressing the problem of evil, had it not been for the hardness of the human heart. In Jesus, God deals with evil on a *spiritual* plane, not just on the physical side of the equation. When Jesus appeared in flesh and blood, he opened a way to attack the source of evil—the hardened human heart, which had been impacted and controlled by the forces of darkness that inspire evil actions.[30]

The work of Jesus Christ made a way to eliminate the bad *from* people, thereby removing the need to eliminate bad people. He introduced a way to fight evil *directly*—to cut it at the "root," not just at the point of its "fruit."[31] Now people could be transformed, "born again"[32]—their hardened hearts changed. Speaking of this day, God promised:

Jesus Christ made a way to eliminate the bad *from* people, thereby removing the need to eliminate bad people.

> I'll give you a new heart, put a new spirit in you. I'll remove the stone heart from your body and replace it with a heart that's God-willed, not self-willed. I'll put my Spirit in you and make it possible for you to do what I tell you and live by my commands. . . . You'll be my people! I'll be your God![33]

Jesus said we no longer have to "resist him who is evil." Why? Because we can attack evil directly. Now the one "caught in adultery" can go free instead of being stoned. And in the act of setting that person free, the power of the adultery itself is exhausted and the adulterer can "go, and sin no more."[34] The miracle of the cross opened the way for God to separate people from the evil they do. No longer do we need to deal violently with hardened souls. Those days are over. Souls can now be "saved."[35]

The miracle of the cross opened the way for God to separate people from the evil they do.

This is why in the New Testament we don't see God sending people to war. "We are not fighting against flesh-and-blood enemies, but against evil rulers and authorities of the unseen world, against mighty powers in this dark world, and against evil spirits in the heavenly places."[36] Yes, we still are in a struggle, a battle; but the war is not against people with evil views or practices. Our warring is no longer against flesh and blood, but against the forces that keep hearts hard and motivate people to do things we believe are evil.[37]

>>A NEW KIND OF WARFARE

Even though we no longer physically attack people who do evil (like they did in the Old Testament), that does not mean we are to passively allow evil to run over us. I don't believe God wants us to think our warring days are over! We are still to be men and women of war. The difference between those who battled in the Old Testament and those called to battle in the New Testament is *how* and with *whom* we battle.

Scripture outlines God's simple, high-octane battle plan against evil in four words: "Overcome evil with good."[38]

That's a plan? you might ask. It certainly lacks bluster. It's not very manly. It sounds weak—even equivocating and vacillating; more like retreat than attack.

Yet, "overcome evil with good" is the plan.

Never mind that it sounds like words from one of the posters hippies put on the walls of their ashrams in the 1960s. Never mind that few believe in that stuff any longer. Never mind that this is the real world, the post-9/11 world.

"Overcome evil with good" is the plan.

But, you might protest, *evil is real. Can something as idealistic as doing good make a dent in the evil that is destroying our world? Does the plan work?*

Yes, it does. Jesus' way works. As believers, Christians are called to enter the war against evil in a new way: where they dare to die, to suffer, to sacrifice as they act kindly toward others. This is the way of the cross, and it has been transforming the world for over two thousand years!

Catherine Marshall related the story of a Lutheran pastor she met in Austria. He was a former Nazi storm trooper who had been radically transformed by nonviolent kindness:

> In December 1941 the trooper was with the German armies invading Russia. In the Crimea, in heavily wooded terrain, the battle began going against the Germans. As they had to fall back, the German found himself within the Russian lines, separated from his regiment. Alone, he made his way through the forest, fearful at every minute of being captured. Suddenly, he saw a thin cloud of smoke coming from the chimney of a hut. Creeping up warily,

gun in hand, he knocked on the door. It was answered by a tiny elderly Russian woman.

Shoving past her and searching the hut, he satisfied himself that the woman lived alone. Apparently, her menfolk were off fighting—perhaps had already been killed. To the German's surprise, the woman offered him food and drink. Neither spoke a word of the other's language, but in the end the Russian woman hid the soldier, feeding him and caring for him for three days and nights. The German grew increasingly baffled. Certainly, no worse enemy than he, a Nazi, could have come to the door here in Russia, where Germans murdered more civilians than the total number of Jews killed in all of Europe. The woods swarmed with Russian troops; surely she knew that if she were caught harboring a German she would be shot.

Out of his mounting desire to communicate, he managed through sign language and facial expressions to convey his question, 'Why have you risked your life to hide and befriend me?'

The old woman looked at him for a long moment in silence, then turned and pointed to a crucifix on the wall above her bed.

Telling me the incident the Lutheran pastor added, "After I escaped back to the German lines, try as I would, I couldn't forget what happened. I hadn't known love like that was possible. In the end, I was drawn irresistibly to the One who enabled that little Russian lady to prefer another to herself—even when the other was a cruel and deadly enemy. I wanted to know the power of the Cross in my life too. That's why I am a Christian today."[39]

Good really does overcome evil. Love and kindness conquer evil by transforming the lives of its carriers. Imagine a world where believers come out fighting evil with love-guns blazin'; a world where Christ followers put others ahead of self and enter a new kind of warfare; a world where the cross is allowed to work its change in hard hearts. This is the way God wanted to fight evil to begin with, but it wasn't possible until he had access to soften the human heart. Jesus made that happen.

>>TO TELL THE TRUTH

The war on evil is waged not merely with kindness, love, forgiveness, and sacrifice, but also with truthtelling. One thinks of Dietrich Bonhoeffer here. During the rise of the Nazi regime, he exhorted Christians to resist evil through exposing and calling attention to the demonic and idolatrous nature of Hitler's effort. This ultimately got him and others killed. Truthtelling also nailed Jesus to the cross. He told the Jewish ruling authorities that they had abdicated their calling as the elect and would finally be judged. Truthtelling is also what ultimately got the early Christians persecuted. It wasn't just that they were compassionate and nice; it was that they were compassionate and nice in the name of the One whose lordship surpassed that of Caesar's. And they talked honestly about it. When the Caesars of Rome realized this, they viciously attacked the followers of Jesus.

The war on evil is waged not merely with love, but also with truthtelling.

So, full-orbed spiritual warfare against, say, racial hatred toward African Americans, might include: (a) concrete acts of love, kindness, and reconciliation with the black community; (b) concrete acts of love directed toward the perpetrators of that hatred; and (c) an honest, public assessment of the evil of racism, including courageous statements about specific acts that particular groups of people have committed. Truthtelling is essential to the war on evil.

>>WHEN VIOLENCE IS APPROPRIATE

Remember, the hardness of people's hearts forced God to treat them directly. Though we are living on this side of the cross, and even though God prefers to overcome the evil in others with good, some folks have become, in the apostle Peter's words, "like brute beasts, creatures of instinct, born only to be caught and destroyed."[40] Some are too hardened and brutal to listen, and they still need to be stopped (criminals, terrorists, rogue states, and the like). How do we deal with them?

The answer is force. There are times when force must still be used against people, even after the cross. Paul addresses this when he talks about how the Old Testament law still has teeth for those not open to grace: "For the law was not intended for people who do what is right. It is for people who are lawless and rebellious, who are ungodly and sinful, who consider nothing sacred and defile what is holy, who kill their father or mother or commit other murders."[41]

Listen carefully as Paul addresses thc role of government:

> Everyone must submit to governing authorities. For all authority comes from God, and those in positions of authority have been placed there by God. So anyone who

> rebels against authority is rebelling against what God has instituted, and they will be punished. For the authorities do not strike fear in people who are doing right, but in those who are doing wrong. Would you like to live without fear of the authorities? Do what is right, and they will honor you. The authorities are God's servants, sent for your good. But if you are doing wrong, of course you should be afraid, for they have the power to punish you. They are God's servants, sent for the very purpose of punishing those who do what is wrong. So you must submit to them, not only to avoid punishment, but also to keep a clear conscience.[42]

Governments are "God's servants" sent to punish those who do wrong. Jesus knew this, of course. During his time here when he spoke to soldiers and officers of government, he never asked a soldier to put down his arms and become nonviolent. Why? Because Jesus knew that some folks are so calloused that the only way to deal with them is with force. (Once they are restrained, they can be treated lovingly, like anyone else.) This is why there should be trials and punishment for criminals. This is also why there has been a long tradition in Christian thought about what is now referred to as the Just War Doctrine. This doctrine states that there are times when military force is considered legitimate and sanctioned by God. But there are strict conditions for that sanction, which include: (a) the damage inflicted by the aggressor on the nation or community of nations must be lasting, grave, and certain; (b) all other nonviolent means of putting an end to the conflict must have been shown to be impractical or ineffective; (c) there must be serious prospects of success by the aggressor; (d) the use of arms must not produce evils and disorders graver than the evil that is trying to be eliminated.[43] Those with the power to use modern means of destruction must carefully weigh these conditions when considering their options.

>>RADICAL ENGAGEMENT

Precisely because God is *not* a bully, he lets us go our own way. Consequently, our culture has lost sight of God. Far from honoring God, it honors things like wealth, self, pleasure, personal advantage, comfort, convenience, status, and making it to the top. As society drifts farther from God and his ways, the face of evil comes into clearer focus. Evildoers seem bolder than ever; they no longer hide their tactics. Celebrities build careers out of doing the things they would have kept secret a generation ago. Evil is now public. It's praised and rewarded. It's something to be aspired to, not kept under wraps. Evil is right there in front of us. What do Christians do in response?

They are to live differently—radically by some standards. Jesus calls his followers to stop living lives committed to self. Instead they are to embrace obedience, sacrifice, simplicity, humility, holiness, kindness, patience, goodness, self-control—all while heralding the truth in love. This kind of living creates a question in the minds of those who experience it, and Christian influence begins.

> God loves to use small things to change the world.

It's not that Christians are perfect or that they have the answers for all the problems of the world. Instead, Christians are called to live in the hope that God loves to use small things to change the world. Every person can be part of building a different, better world. Our union with God influences situations, community, family, friendships, work—*everything*.

Sadly, many of us who are Christ followers, try to hide from evil by retreating into Christian enclaves; others try to crush evil by pulling out bullhorns and using whatever power they can grab to coerce conformity and impose rules. Both paths are incongruent with Jesus' instructions. It doesn't matter who we are or where we've been. God uses grandpas and moms, plumbers and neurosurgeons, ex-cons and seminarians, sanitation workers and Starbucks managers. God longs for *all* of us to participate in overcoming evil with good and to be a part of building a different, better world.

God is not finished with planet Earth. And he wants to use us to fight with him in the war against the evil that appears here. There is much desperation in our world and a long struggle lies ahead of us. But we have the one weapon that overwhelms desperation: *hope*. Paul wrote, "Hope does not disappoint."[44] Hope pushes us beyond the limits of a fallen world into the kingdom that will have no end.

08

>>A MISUSE OF SCRIPTURE

it bothers me that believers consistently misuse sacred text

"The abomination that causes desolation?"[1] Jim read with a questioning tone. Then he looked up and asked, "What in the world is that?"

We were all novices at Bible interpretation, but we had decided to wrestle through the prophetic Bible verses on the end times. It was a free-for-all.

A couple of us took a stab at possible meanings for "the abomination that causes desolation." No one even suggested we look at the historical or textual contexts the verse was nestled in. We tried to figure out what it meant through the lens of modernity.

A guy visiting our group for the first time piped right in. "The Lord has shown me what this means." (It's always more interesting when God himself weighs in on an interpretation!) We all looked at him with anticipation. "I've discovered that it is helpful to break words apart when you study Scripture," he said with all seriousness. "If you break down 'abomination,' you get *a-bom-in-nation*. This verse is a prediction that a number of nations would one day get the *atomic bomb*. And it's happening," he exclaimed with lots of excitement. "We are in the last days!"

The fact that this story even happened makes me wonder if the Bible should come with a warning label slapped on its cover: *If you are already kind of nuts, this book will only make things worse.* In one sense I'm thankful the Scriptures are accessible to so many, and yet it bothers me that folks treat it like a purely existential document that should be interpreted through each reader's peculiar point of view.

>>THE GOOD, THE BAD, AND THE UGLY

I love the Bible. It's full of narrative history, genealogies, laws, poetry, proverbs, prophetic oracles, riddles, drama, biographical sketches, parables, letters, sermons, and apocalypses. I want to say it's magical, but some of my evangelical brothers and sisters would get nervous. It is definitely a mystical book that fills the believing heart with life, wonder, grace, power, and comfort. All Christian believers treasure the Bible. It has been the best-selling book in the world since printing began. When Gutenberg invented the printing press, the first words he reproduced were the words of the Bible.

However, giving people the impression that the Bible is easy to understand and easy to apply is really a disservice. That's like saying marriage is easy. Certainly marriage can be wonderful, but it is *not* easy. It is not easy to keep your "I" on your spouse and off yourself. It is not easy for men to understand women, and vice versa. Neither is it easy to understand the Bible. Often, it is very difficult. Some texts seem impossible to comprehend. That is why, throughout history, so many have used the Bible for their own, sometimes horrible purposes.

It is hard to imagine, but the sacred Scriptures, which have brought unspeakable comfort and blessing to countless millions, have also been used to bring pain, horror, and death to many. The Bible was used to validate the torture of so-called heretics, to justify slavery, to oppress women, and to perpetuate other travesties.

The sacred Scriptures, which have brought unspeakable comfort and blessing to countless millions, have also been used to bring pain, horror, and death.

On a less disturbing but equally ridiculous note, believers throughout history have used the Bible to "prove" specifically *when* Jesus Christ would return. (I guess Jesus never got any of their memos.)

When faced with the possibility of war, one group of believers has used Scripture to prove we should go to war, while those on the other side of the ideological aisle have used the same Bible to prove we are never supposed to go to war.

How can this be? How can there be such divergent thought about the "truth"?

Some would argue that the Bible doesn't need interpretation; it just needs to be obeyed. In some cases that is true. Paul commands, "Do everything without complaining or arguing."[2] That doesn't need interpretation; it needs obedience, plain and simple.

But not all texts are that simple. And if we are not careful, we can think our understanding of what we read is the meaning that the Holy Spirit intended. But that is a huge assumption, and it ignores that our experiences, the culture we live in, our prior understanding of words and ideas, and so on, always inject themselves into what we read. We are kidding ourselves if we think our biases cannot lead us astray and cause us to read unintended ideas into the text.

Case in point: Let's say you grew up believing it is wrong for people to get tattoos and have their bodies pierced. Maybe you heard your mom and dad say it was wrong. Or perhaps you believe that because, when you were growing up, tattoos and body piercings were only fashionable for mean-looking bikers, biker chicks, and those on the low end of the socioeconomic scale. Is that an unfair prejudice? Yeah. But if that was your experience, it impacts how you think.

Our experience and the culture we live in always inject themselves into what we read.

Whatever the reason, inbred opinions cause us to read Bible texts with a predetermined selectivity. We come across a verse such as, "Do not cut your bodies . . . or put tattoo marks on yourselves. I am the Lord,"[3] and it leaps off the page to us. And when an internal resonance occurs, it can feel much like a spiritual epiphany—like the voice of God. *No wonder tattoos and piercings trouble us so*, we reason. *God feels that same way!* Never mind that in the previous verse men are told never "cut the hair at the sides of your head or clip off the edges of your beard."[4] Christians ignore that verse. But if they choose to obey the command that forbids tattoos or piercings, reason demands that they obey this one too, which means churches would be full of men with mullets and scraggly, untrimmed beards.

So why aren't Christians fair and reasonable when it comes to interpreting Bible texts like these? Because something in each of us longs to emphasize the things that resonate with our own opinions and biases, while ignoring the ones that don't. However, it's one thing to interpret Bible texts in a biased, squirrelly way; it's quite another to slap God's endorsement on our interpretation. But people do it every day. No wonder atheists and agnostics ridicule the way Christians use the Bible.

We don't need to do that. If we don't like something, we just need to be honest about it. For instance, Gail and I do not personally like tattoos or body piercings. As our four kids grew, we told them tattoos and piercings were not allowed in the Gungor house. We said, with smiles on our faces, "It isn't that God is against it. In fact, he has tattoos. He has *us* tattooed on his hand.[5] Apparently, he's *into* tattoos. It's that your mom and dad are against it. We don't want you permanently altering your body until you are an adult and decide to do so. We're just weird, old-fashioned parents. Get used to it."

It's one thing to interpret Bible texts in a biased, squirrelly way; it's quite another to slap God's endorsement on our interpretation.

It's okay for parents to be uptight about some stuff. We just can't project our preferences onto God and "swear . . . by heaven"[6] that God feels the same way.

It's not that we can't have unreasonably conservative opinions about things—we just need to own that all of us have BluBlocker vision that affects how we see things.

>>BLUBLOCKERS

Back in the 1980s there was a huge promotion for BluBlocker sunglasses. They boasted of providing UV and blue-light protection for the eyes. I sported a pair of those unisex "as-seen-on-TV" sunglasses with a large degree of misguided pride.

One day my family and I were heading out of town, and we stopped to fill up with gas and grab some treats from the quick mart. Gail asked me to get her some of her favorite gum. I always recognized her gum by the color of the package. She liked the Wrigley's kind in the big blue pack. I grabbed it, paid, and brought it back to the car.

We were heading down the road when she asked, "Why didn't you get me my regular kind?"

"I did," I answered.

"No, you didn't," she said as she pointed to the pack.

I took the gum, held it up, and said rather sarcastically, "Gail, the pack is blue. This is the kind you like!"

She paused for a second and said, "Take off the BluBlockers, Eddie."

I reached up and pulled off the glasses and realized I had inadvertently purchased the green gum, thinking I was purchasing the blue gum. Something in the BluBlockers made the green pack look blue.

What looks true sometimes isn't, and what looks untrue is sometimes true.

That's what happens to us when our lives get colored by our experience and we interpret our surroundings through that color. That means what looks true sometimes isn't, and what looks untrue is sometimes true. Our ideas, presuppositions, and even prejudices color our reasoning and interpretive skills. We don't see clearly.

People have been wearing BluBlockers all through history. For example, in the premodern world a violent natural event like an earthquake or an erupting volcano was thought of as some kind of vengeance from the gods. Their BluBlocker was that they believed gods did that sort of thing. When there was a natural disaster, people assumed someone had killed a sacred animal or had committed some heinous crime that angered the gods and the cataclysmic event was retribution for that immoral act.

In the modern world, we know natural disasters brew because of a number of natural conditions. This is our BluBlocker. What premoderns saw as acts of the gods, moderns see as the logical result of nature's adjustments. No vengeance here.

Different BluBlockers lead to different interpretations.

In my small hometown in rural Wisconsin, I knew a woman who believed there was no way the United States ever got those men on the moon—not really. When asked about the live television broadcasts that captured the event, she would say, "It was all Hollywood. They staged the whole thing. It was fake, and a lot of people made a lot of money from our tax dollars." Her BluBlocker conspiracy "glasses" made the whole thing appear to be a hoax. People who view the world as conspiratorial or interpret biblical prophecy by breaking the words apart (especially since Scripture was originally written in Hebrew and Greek—not English) are wearing bad BluBlockers. When we use faulty methods or tools to interpret something, the world ends up looking distorted and weird.

When we use faulty methods or tools to interpret something, the world ends up looking distorted and weird.

The BluBlockers we wear provide a framework for processing data, just like prescription eyeglasses frame what we (who need them) see. I remember getting my first pair of eyeglasses as a kid and being amazed at how it helped me see the world in a whole new way—clearly. I had become used to the blur.

Sadly, there are many disorienting "prescription" BlueBlockers out there. Instead of clearing things up, they actually distort and give us an inaccurate view of the world. There is no place where this is truer than in the context of religion. When it comes to what we believe about God (theology), how we think he wants us to live (doctrines), and what we can or cannot do (commandments and injunctions), Christians have so many different sets of glasses, we make Elton John's eyewear collection seem paltry.

All kinds of things influence the way we see things: our experiences, our parents, Dr. Phil, our friends, the churches we've attended, *The Matrix*, our prejudices, expectations, hopes, failures, God, the devil, being American, an *Oprah* show we once saw—these all color the way we interpret our world and our faith.

Let's look at some common, but bad, BluBlockers Christians wear today.

>>LEGALIST BLUBLOCKERS

The Pharisees were the religious leaders of Jesus' day. You would think they would have been the good guys. They kept all the rules, many of which they made up! They *seemed* to be trying to do what was right. But Jesus didn't see it that way. In fact, the Pharisees were the only group he openly campaigned against.

In Jesus' preaching, he never came against the prostitutes, thieves, drunkards, or tax collectors (the closest thing to organized crime in Israel at the time). He befriended folks from those crowds. But he was completely at odds with the ministry of the Pharisees. Jesus consistently warned his followers to "beware of," to "be careful" about, and to "watch out" for the teachings and lifestyle of these guys. The Pharisees were the Eagle Scouts of religion. And they were sporting some pretty thick BluBlockers.

Fence Laws

It's difficult to catch the error of Pharisaic reasoning, because it begins with the Word of God. The problem wasn't in their desire to keep God's laws, but in the strategy they employed for keeping them. Jesus said of them: "Instead of giving you God's Law as food and drink by which you can banquet on God, they package it in bundles of rules, loading you down like pack animals."[7] The Pharisees actually *added* to God's law, and it was the bundle of rules they added that made Pharisaic thinking dangerous. The additional rules became known as *fence laws*.

To ensure that a specific law of God was obeyed, the Pharisees believed they should make up rules that "fenced" people a step back from breaking the actual command. They thought of these fence laws as a first line of defense against disobedience. They reasoned that if a person had to break a manmade fence law before breaking one of God's real laws, the fence law would be a deterrent and a protection for people. Noble enough.

The Pharisees believed they should make up rules that "fenced" people a step back from breaking the actual command.

But the Pharisees ended up creating hundreds of fence laws, dealing with everything from what one could wear or eat, to what one could or couldn't do on the Sabbath and with whom. So whether you wanted to pray, fast, rest, or whatever, there were dozens of rules to follow.

The problem was, there were too many rules to keep track of, much less follow. It wasn't possible to obey them all unless you devoted yourself to rehearsing and obeying them, which meant you had to become a Pharisee. There was no way the average illiterate Jewish person could keep up with these guys. So the masses did the best they could and then pretty much resigned themselves to the fact that they were lost, unholy sinners. And the Pharisees gloated. They loved being the only holy ones in Israel.

The Pharisees saw religious rules as a kind of God language. And they were the only ones who spoke it! They believed the more rules a person knew, the more he or she would be able to commune with God. They thought their manmade rituals, formulas, and rules brought people closer to God. But the truth was, their additions served to "nullify" the simple, true commands of God.[8]

But the Pharisees were not the only ones who created fence laws. The practice has been passed down through the centuries and into today.

Modern Legalistic Fences

Let's take a moment to look at how fence laws are created. Analogous to our discussion would be parents who love their children and build fence laws for them. Take the rule "Don't get hit by a car." Good rule. If you think about this rule long enough—and you believe you must do everything possible to ensure it will be obeyed—you might be tempted to bundle another rule to it, to add a "fence" that can serve as the first line of defense so that the actual rule you are ultimately trying to enforce doesn't get violated.

A logical fence law added to "Don't get hit by a car" would be "Don't play in the street." If you don't play in the street, a car certainly won't hit you. That's a reasonable addition.

But pharisaic thinking goes way beyond reasonableness and gets much more restrictive. Modern pharisaic thinking would go something like this: *The rule is, "Don't get hit by a car." We cannot allow anyone to be hit by a car . . . so, let's make sure that doesn't happen. Let's start by forbidding anyone from playing in the street—no street play will mean no one is hit by a car. Or better yet, it's probably best not to play outside* at all, *because then you won't happen into the street to get hit by a car. Or even better: don't look out the windows of the house, lest you are tempted to think about going outside, which could lead you to wandering into the street to get hit by a car. Or perhaps best of all: play and sleep in the closet so you aren't tempted to look out a window at all—because you know where that can lead . . .*

At what point do the fence laws obscure what the original law was all about? And that was the problem with the Pharisees' fence laws. They eventually overwhelmed the actual commands of God. Jesus said to the Pharisees, "You have a fine way of setting aside the commands of God in order to observe your own traditions."[9]

But more than just distracting from God's law, fence laws also became abusive. At what point does the legitimate desire to protect become a repressive system of abuse? Parents who make their kids live in closets need to go to jail. It doesn't matter if they started out loving, concerned, and protective. These parents ended up being controlling, manipulative, and repressive. That's Jesus' point about the Pharisees. The fence laws became weights that crippled rather than strengthened faith. Legalism is a crushing BluBlocker.

> At what point does the legitimate desire to protect become a repressive system of abuse?

Sadly, church folks are still wearing pharisaic BluBlocker glasses today. For example, the Bible commands us not to get "drunk" with wine. A simple, clear command. But instead of preaching about drinking in moderation, many groups add the fence law of never drinking a drop of alcohol *at all*—total abstinence. This is so pervasive in evangelical churches in America that most of them use grape juice for Holy Communion instead of the traditional wine. We evangelicals can't use the biblical language of bread and wine; it's bread and *juice.* Nothing wrong with this choice, but it is a human fence law, not God's. Still, for a number of groups, the total abstinence fence isn't enough. Not nearly.

To ensure complete holiness, they add additional fence laws, such as: "Don't even go into restaurants that serve alcohol." Or some modify this law: "You can go to a restaurant that serves liquor, as long as they don't have an open bar." I know of churches that chastise members if they are seen eating at a restaurant that sports an open bar. The "do not get drunk" command of God is eclipsed by the "don't eat at *that* restaurant" rule. And we cannot intelligently answer our kids when they ask, "Why can't we eat at that cool restaurant?"

The more faith is about keeping human rules, the more lifeless it becomes.

I believe people have good intentions when they make rules like this. But the more faith is about keeping human rules, the more lifeless it becomes. That's the position Jesus took. Faith can easily stop being about God and his guidance in our lives and become more about the opinions of others and how they think we should live. It can quickly become a dead, human, religious thing.

Fashion Fences

The Bible clearly warns us against worldliness, which is loving this world and its accoutrements more than loving God and his kingdom.

I met Pastor Joe while I was in high school back in the early 1970s. I had given my life to Christ about two years before but still wore the clothes and hairstyle that were popular for my generation. And Pastor Joe was concerned. Pastor Joe was an old-school conservative who felt that worldliness could be best avoided by a couple of fence laws that would preempt one from going down the worldliness path.

"I'm concerned about you, Ed," he told me as he pulled me aside one day. "I feel like you are still carrying the marks of worldliness. The Scriptures tell us to 'love not the world, neither the things that are in the world.' "[10] He continued, quoting exclusively from the King James text. "And I fear you are in love with the world."

"Why do you think that?" I asked, confused because I had sold out for God in my heart.

"Why, look at how you are dressed—and your hair," he answered. "You look like a hippie. You are communicating rebellion, sexual promiscuity, and drug usage everywhere you go."

Clothing and hairstyles do not necessarily reflect what is going on in the heart.

The truth is, clothing and hairstyles do not necessarily reflect what is going on in the heart. I was certainly not dressing lewdly (remember the baggy-legged, disheveled hippie look of the 1970s?), and although in Pastor Joe's mind I looked like I was associated with drug addiction and youthful rebellion, I was just dressing the way kids my age dressed.

He went on to ask me, "Don't you admit that what we wear speaks to people?"

"I guess," I replied.

"Well, what do you think your clothing is speaking, versus what I am wearing?" he asked.

"I think my clothing is saying, 'I like to be comfortable,'" I told him. But he wasn't buying it. He told me I needed to wear what he was wearing.

Pastor Joe always wore dark pants; black shoes; a pressed, white shirt; and a plain, dark tie. He would have looked like a character in *The Blues Brothers*, but he had a 1961 haircut, so he wasn't nearly as cool.

I told him I couldn't imagine wearing what he had on. I didn't say much more than that, but I couldn't help but think that the way he dressed was "speaking" that he was an extra from *Leave It to Beaver*. I also knew that if I tried to dress like him, my friends would have thought I believed it was Halloween.

It's been over thirty-five years since that conversation, and I still run into people who, like Pastor Joe, believe that being fashionable is worldliness. I guess they reason that if they are fashionless, they will never get anywhere near becoming worldly. Hence, if you want to see what was in style a few years ago, just watch some Christian television or visit a few old school evangelical or Pentecostal churches this Sunday. These groups often contend by example that being out of sync with style is a mark of holiness.

God says nothing about fashion and clothing styles in the Bible.

Other than a call to general modesty, God says nothing about fashion and clothing styles in the Bible. He does warn us about loving this world too much. But does that translate into wearing clothing that is eight to ten years out of style? Don't think so. Bad BluBlockers.

The words of Jesus come to mind:

> You're hopeless, you religion scholars and Pharisees! Frauds! You keep meticulous account books, tithing on every nickel and dime you get, but on the meat of God's Law, things like fairness and compassion and commitment—the absolute basics!—you carelessly take it or leave it. Careful bookkeeping is commendable, but the basics are required. Do you have any idea how silly you look, writing a life story that's wrong from start to finish, nitpicking over commas and semicolons?[11]

>>FUNDAMENTALIST BLUBLOCKERS

I believe that the Bible is the inerrant Word of God, which means I believe it is perfectly accurate in its present form. Now, the fundamentalists have taken that to mean that the Bible is to be taken *literally* at all times. But that is another bad BluBlocker. Remember that the Bible is a divine library, filled with history, law, poetry, songs, stories, letters, parables, drama, philosophy, sermons—and more. Don't try to take every word literally.

Truth is, the fundamentalists who claim they do so are lying. Just ask them if they take Psalm 18:2 literally, "The LORD is my rock, my fortress and my deliverer." Do they really believe God is a "rock," or do they think that the word *rock* is metaphorical? They will answer metaphorical, which proves they are not true literalists. How does one decide what is metaphorical and what is literal in the Bible?

Like all of us, fundamentalists make their decisions about what is literal and what is not based on their own biases. Classic example: the Bible commands people to "Greet one another with a holy kiss."[12] Seems simple enough. Certainly doesn't seem metaphorical. So, why don't the literalists obey this command? Five times we are commanded directly: "Greet one another with a holy kiss."[13] If fundamentalists take the Bible literally, why not just obey it? Why doesn't everyone start greeting one another with a holy kiss at church and when they meet in public? American men could eventually get used to kissing other men. It would make us stick out if we did this—perhaps it could be a witnessing tool? It's God's command from his inerrant Word, right? Don't fundamentalists believe the Bible? Apparently not. Literal, fundamentalist, Bible absolutists will argue that texts like these need to be filtered through the context of the culture in which they were written.

Like all of us, fundamentalists make their decisions about what is literal and what is not based on their own biases.

But wait a minute.

How can they justify ignoring the commands of certain texts, appealing to the cultural context, while demanding others be obeyed without using the same analysis? Why do they demand obedience only to the texts that resonate with them, while being critical of the ones that seem odd to them? Yep. BluBlockers. In short, some scriptures echo the biases and theological backgrounds of people, making them easily relegated to insignificance.

This is a huge problem in evangelical churches. Many refuse to acknowledge that human pretensions, biases, cultures, and prejudices impact our ability to interpret and understand Scripture. This is why one needs to humbly and suspiciously approach the Bible; readers must cultivate humility in their hearts and be suspicious of their own penchant to wear BluBlockers. They need to acknowledge that a literal reading of the Bible can be a dangerous oversimplification. The true meaning of a biblical text is often more complicated to unearth. Christ followers need to carefully consider the verses that precede and follow the text being studied (many people pull verses right out of their setting and create or support wrong ideas). They need to approach the text by comparing one passage in the light of others that address the same subject. Careful readers will consider and research the time when the text was written and the unique circumstances surrounding that text. The humble Bible student will listen to other voices (books, sermons, historical studies revealing how the church has historically dealt with an issue) and ask good questions like: Who is being spoken to? What did it mean to those present when it was spoken? How do I apply it practicaly in my life?

Christ followers need to be more like my friend Jerry, who is color blind. He tells me that anytime he picks out his own clothes, people stare. When he drives, he must be extra careful—he can't distinguish the red lights from the green. When I heard this, I was surprised. I had never noticed, and I had known Jerry for years. When I mentioned how well he concealed his sight challenge, he said, "That's because I don't trust myself. If I did, you would have known it the day you met me—I would have been the one dressed like a clown. But I learned early that if I don't ask for help, I'm in trouble."

Many in the church should admit that they need help when it comes to negotiating Scripture.

J. I. Packer writes, "approach Scripture with minds already formed by the mass of accepted opinions and viewpoints with which we have come into contact, in both the Church and the world . . . It is easy to be unaware that it has happened; it is hard even to begin to realize how profoundly tradition in this sense has molded us. . . . We may never assume the complete rightness of our own established ways of thought and practice and excuse ourselves the duty of testing and reforming them."[14]

>>LAST-DAYS BLUS

One of the most damaging BluBlockers I have encountered in my thirty years of pastoral care is the last-days BluBlocker. When I first came to Christ, the group I hung with talked a lot about the return of Jesus Christ. We used to pass out fake newspapers with the headline "Christ Returns!" We were sure the event known as the Rapture (where Jesus returns to snatch away his followers) was close—certainly within the next year or two. That was a little over thirty-five years ago.

Last-days prophecy stuff is fascinating and extremely motivating. Thinking about the possible imminent return of Jesus produces amazing commitment and devotion. The apostle John said a person who thinks about it "purifies himself, just as he is pure."[15] The idea that we are going to see Jesus is very cool. His followers will no longer live by faith—they're *really* going to see him!

But there are problems.

Preachers with a penchant for interpreting Bible prophecy hold the daily news in one hand and the Bible in the other.

As far back as you care to go historically, you can find preachers with a penchant for interpreting Bible prophecy by holding the daily news in one hand and the Bible in the other. Using obscure texts and arbitrary methods, many have tried to prove the identity of the Antichrist or discern which country is the nation known as Magog in Scripture (a nation important in last-days prophecy). Back in the 1950s, many last-days pundits claimed Magog was the Soviet Union, but in the 1980s the Soviet Union collapsed. Then new revelations began to come as to the identity of the "true" Magog (many now say Magog is Islam). What bothers me is how the last-days experts talk with such confidence and authority. They don't *suggest* that this or that may happen or say that a verse *might* mean this or that—it is a done deal; their interpretation is absolute truth. And something is always happening in the Middle East or elsewhere that serves as another indication that the return of Jesus is just around the corner.

Not long ago I heard a well-meaning Bible-prophecy radio minister trying to use a cryptic Bible text to prove that Scripture predicted a recent series of terrorist attacks in Israel. These guys read the *New York Times* and the *Jerusalem Post* the way a psychic reads tea leaves. And with a rising fever in the air, you get the feeling you need to stay close and stay tuned to hear the latest from their prophetic perspective. You want to make sure you are ready!

But then, when what they say doesn't happen or the interpretation they have been espousing demands adjustment, they do so as unapologetically and as frequently as the local meteorologist. But are Bible prophecies supposed to be approached like weather forecasts, or should Christians just be a little more tentative about their interpretations to begin with?

Knock, Knock, Who Knows?

If you want to take a trip to a new time zone, just start reading the Bible passages that describe the last days, which you will find in Bible books such as Ezekiel, Daniel, Zechariah, and Isaiah—but especially in the book of Revelation. Within its pages you run into angels, trumpets, earthquakes, biting locusts, beasts, dragons, and bottomless pits. Alice's Wonderland looks tame by comparison.

Why is there so much room for arbitrary interpretation in the arena of Bible prophecy? Primarily because most of it was written in a style (or genre) called apocalyptic literature. This style of writing is not found anywhere else in modern literature, and we have a hard time trying to decipher and interpret it.

To better understand the challenge, imagine being part of an archaeological team one million years from now that uncovers a few "knock, knock" jokes from our century. Let's say you have no counterpart in your culture—no "knock, knock" jokes exist.

You translate the text:

> Knock, knock.
> Who's there?
> Duane.
> Duane who?
> Duane the bathtub,
> I think I'm duowning.

As you try to interpret the writing, someone suggests, "Perhaps the word *knock* has some kind of special meaning. Notice they said it twice." Someone else pipes in and says, "Yes, and apparently Duane is the name of a bathing device—it reads, 'Duane the bathtub.'"

Yet another remarks, "And what do you think 'duowning' is?"

"Perhaps it has something to do with the double 'knock,'" you reply.

Everyone has missed the point.

You might come up with half a dozen equally ridiculous interpretations, simply because you don't understand that this is a joke. Jokes have characteristics that must be understood in order for the joke to make sense. The same kind of thing is true when we are reading apocalyptic literature. I'm not suggesting apocalyptic literature is anything like a joke, but it has certain characteristics that must be understood in order for it to make any sense to us.

Just as stories, parables, and psalms have specific literary characteristics, so does apocalyptic literature. It includes heavy themes of judgment and salvation, jammed with visions and dreams. The language is cryptic and symbolic; the images are often forms of fantasy rather than reality; and time and events are neatly divided and carefully ordered with a great fondness for the symbolic use of numbers. When you take an apocalyptic book like Revelation—which is populated with visions, dreams, cryptic and symbolic language, fantasy, prophecy, and some general epistle, or letter, material—you have the makings of a gnarly piece of literature.

But most Bible readers ignore all those characteristics of apocalyptic literature and approach prophetic texts with an open heart and prayer. It sounds good—spiritual even. But is it? Go ahead and put one hundred people in a room and ask them to take a run at this kind of material prayerfully, with open hearts, and you will end up with one hundred different interpretations. BluBlockers.

Christians should be very suspicious of their understanding of the Scriptures.

Christians should be very suspicious of their understanding of the Scriptures. This is especially true when reading prophetic segments. For example, if you think God directed Bible prophecy toward Americans more than Libyans, Afghans, or Sudanese, then end-times verses will read differently to you. But if you are a Christian from the Sudan (many who are currently having their property seized and their children taken from them), you may think the great tribulation is taking place *now* and that you have already met the armies of the Antichrist.

Honest Bible readers need to be more wary of their last-days interpretations.

Short-Term Yields

Talk about the return of Jesus Christ often gets people motivated to serve. But I would suggest the motivation is not good when people get excited about the return of Christ based on current events that are interpreted hastily and inappropriately. In 1988 a booklet came out titled *88 Reasons Why the Rapture Will Be in 1988*. Tens of thousands of believers bought that little book and made it a central issue in their lives. People I knew were passing the books out to relatives, friends, coworkers, and neighbors. It created quite a stir. I had been around the block a couple of times by 1988, so I wasn't nearly as taken with the idea. I remember telling those I pastored at the time, "Don't get too excited, folks. Jesus said no one would know the exact time or hour of his return! I hate to pop your end-times bubble, but I have some plans for 1989."

Talking about Jesus' return the way Chicken Little talked about the falling sky always yields less-than-favorable results.

When Jesus didn't come back, the author came out with another work with a title to the tune of *89 Reasons Why the Rapture Is in 1989*. It didn't sell nearly as well. People who got all jacked up from the first book were disappointed and embarrassed after Jesus didn't return in 1988. Some even slipped away from the Lord. Why? Talking about Jesus' return the way Chicken Little talked about the falling sky always yields less-than-favorable results.

Instead of forcing obscure texts into modern news stories, wouldn't it be better to spend the energy trying to inspire people to long for Christ's return?

A Healthy Eschatology

When you read the New Testament, you get the idea that the early church expected Jesus to return at any moment—*and that was 2,000 years ago!* Why would those Christians talk about the return of Jesus in a way that suggested it could happen at any moment? I think the answer is found in Paul's comment that God rewards those "who have longed for his appearing."[16] God wants his children to think about, dream about, and long for the return of Jesus Christ.

Honestly, until recently I never did that. I never consciously fostered a longing for the appearing of Jesus. When I first came to him and heard the end-times message, I got excited and was motivated by it—but Jesus didn't come. And because many of the events that were used as evidence that his return was imminent proved no such thing, I got a tad jaded.

Today I long for Christ's return because I want to go home. Before he left, Jesus said, "Do not let your hearts be troubled. . . . I am going . . . to prepare a place for you. . . . I will come back and take you to be with me that you also may be where I am."[17] This planet is not home. At best, it is a hotel room. Longing for the return of Jesus needs to rest on the footing that he has made a home for believers and is coming to get them—not based on some prophecy expert's dubious revelation. It is said of the saints of old, "they were longing for a better country—a heavenly one. Therefore God is not ashamed to be called their God, for he has prepared a city for them."[18]

Go ahead and peek through that set of BluBlockers.

>>REPUBLICAN BLUBLOCKERS

Another example of BluBlockers that has given Christians a bad name has to do with faith and politics. Something in me wants to believe God is a Republican. I'm a Republican. I like the idea of smaller government and less taxes, and I think the abortion and gay-rights agendas have gained too much ground. I used to believe my political preferences were the result of what I have read in the Bible, certainly not fashioned by my upper-middle-class upbringing. Then I met some folks who helped me see I was wearing BluBlockers.

I used to believe my political preferences were the result of what I have read in the Bible.

I was preaching in a large evangelical church in St. Louis, Missouri—right after President Clinton and the Democrats won the White House. As were all good Republicans, I was depressed and downcast. And, like most evangelicals, I presumed God was as well. In my message that Sunday morning, I lamented the loss of the election and decried the agenda of abortion and gay rights that was sure to gain greater footing in our culture under the Democratic watch.

Immediately after the service, a handsome, astute couple approached me. The woman spoke up: "Pastor Gungor," she said, "I have always enjoyed and appreciated your ministry here, but this morning I am afraid you have offended me."

"I'm sorry," I replied. "What exactly did I do?"

"Have you ever had a son or daughter or a niece or nephew murdered in a drive-by shooting?"

"No," I responded, a little puzzled.

"How would you like to tuck your daughter into an iron bathtub on Saturday nights just to protect her from that sort of thing?"

"I wouldn't like that," I replied sheepishly.

"Do the majority of young boys in your neighborhood get strung out on drugs or get into gangs?" she asked further.

"No," I answered, realizing where she was going.

"I certainly agree with you that God is against abortion and homosexuality, but are those the *only* sins God is concerned with? Are you suggesting that God doesn't care about the murders of innocent children through drive-by shootings in the inner city or the destruction of young lives through gangs and drugs? Are those sins of less concern to God, or do you suppose they are just of less concern to folks like you, who have been insulated and isolated from the concerns that befall those of us in the urban jungle?"

I knew the questions were rhetorical and her tone passionate, so I just humbly continued to listen.

"The Democratic Party may not resolve the issues that plague the inner city," she continued, "but at least they are willing to talk about them and listen to those of us who do care. Because of that, we certainly don't agree with you that the victory of the Democratic Party was, in any way, a loss for the kingdom of God. And we don't feel it was appropriate for you to suggest that people of faith should feel the way you do."

I was stunned. I apologized and walked away, embarrassed that I did not have the crimes that ravage the inner city on my ethical or moral radar screen. What if I lived in a neighborhood ravaged by drugs and violence? What if my own daughter had to sleep in a bathtub at night? Would I be as concerned about gay rights or abortion advocates? Would I vote differently?

James said, "For whoever obeys the whole of God's law and yet stumbles at just one point is guilty, period. For the one who said, 'Do not commit adultery,' is also the one who said, 'Do not murder.' If you break one rule, you break them all."[19] In other words, sin is sin.

I am still a Republican, and I vote Republican because I believe that the most long-term benefit to America will be garnered by the philosophy espoused by the Republican agenda. However, I am now more sympathetic to those of a contrary position. In all honesty, neither party is completely right. For example, the Democrats' solution to poverty seems to focus more on immediate, right-now help. Republicans argue that right-now help creates problems—it overburdens the taxpayers and creates a crippling dependency. I personally agree more with the Republican solution to poverty: education. Education encourages independence and responsibility. Over the long haul, a good education will empower people to secure better lives. But tell that to a poor inner-city first grader who is going to bed hungry tonight because her single parent has lost her job! This child will not be all that excited about the Republican solution. I'm not sure the parent will be either.

In all honesty, neither party is completely right.

Bottom line is, at this point in my life I am not nearly as prone to homogenize my evangelical faith with my political-party affiliation. Nor am I as quick to judge those who vote Democratic. I don't assume they are pro-gay and pro-choice any more than I want them to assume I am greedy and uncompassionate just because some Republicans have a reputation for being that way.

At this point in my life I am not nearly as prone to homogenize my evangelical faith with my political-party affiliation.

Perhaps we should all just vote our convictions and leave the results in the hands of God. Maybe we should dare believe that "the Most High is sovereign over the kingdoms of men and gives them to anyone he wishes."[20]

>>GOOD BLUBLOCKERS

Just as you can have negative "rose-colored" BluBlockers, you can also wear some very positive ones. Jesus wore several sets of good BluBlockers. Christians would have a much more positive impact on the world if they wore the lenses Jesus did. One of Jesus' BluBlockers saw the goodness of God everywhere. When he looked at things like the sunshine or rain, he saw God's goodness. When speaking about God's incautious goodness to humanity he said, "Your Father in heaven . . . causes his sun to rise on the evil and the good, and sends rain on the righteous and the unrighteous."[21]

Another good pair of BluBlockers Christians should wear is knowing that God's love is everywhere. God is lovingly chasing us even when there is no good reason to do so. When the psalmist caught a glimpse of the love and favor God had for him, he cried, "This is too much, too wonderful—I can't take it all in!"[22] Neither can we.

God's love may resemble the natural kindness and love that families and married couples share; but it plunges far deeper, and it is way more unconditional and deathless. This kind of love is so "out of the box" for human understanding that Paul prayed his friends would have the "power to understand, as all God's people should, how wide, how long, how high, and how deep his love is."[23] It takes "power to understand" God's love and grace toward us; God has to help us see it.

I totally get how some think all this is too good to be true. How can God be so reckless about giving to us when we are so good at being so bad? But that is exactly what he is like. We matter to him, and there is nothing we can do to alter that. Now that's a sweet pair of BluBlockers.

> I totally get how some think all this is too good to be true.

One of my favorite BluBlockers is knowing that God made each one of us on purpose. The Bible claims that before time—in eternity—God imagined every individual. This means he manipulated the odds through history to make sure *you* got here. Scripture asserts that God started from the first humans and chose the "times set" for each of us to appear in history and the "exact places" where we would be born![24] The psalmist declared, "All the days ordained for me were written in your book before one of them came to be."[25] To God, this isn't a land for the "survival of the fittest"—it is a world for the predestined. He picked us. And he has a plan for us. This means you were a forethought in God's mind, you are not here by chance, and, in a very real way, you are a dream come true for God. This also means that the other folks in our world—whether they agree with us about God or not—are also here by design.

Scripture goes so far as to say God managed your growth while you were in your mother's womb[26]—your physicality and unique blend of personality were created *on purpose.* You were chosen to show up on this planet. The Christian story claims you and I are *not* accidents; we are on-purpose beings that God placed in the world as unique characters in his unfolding story. Walking in life looking through this set of BluBlockers will change the tone of your life and impact how you live and how you feel about yourself.

You are not here by chance, and, in a very real way, you are a dream come true for God.

If Christians approached the world with these good BluBlockers on, not only would their own views be better, but those who encounter them would have a much clearer picture of who God *really* is.

>>SOME GENERAL ENCOURAGEMENTS

Here are some general encouragements that will keep Christians from misusing sacred text:

Be a Student

A great number of study aids are available in bookstores and online to help one steer safely into a clearer biblical understanding. Search some of these out. Read different Bible translations. Always remember, there are lots of spiritual weirdos, so try to study books by writers who stay close to doctrines that have survived for centuries. Be especially wary of people who say, "God told me this means . . ." God *may* have spoken to them, but you should test what they say.[27] The Bible says, "there is nothing new under the sun."[28] If God told them, he has told others also. Make sure trusted "others" throughout history say the same thing.

Embrace Paradox

The Bible contains paradoxes. A paradox is a seemingly contradictory statement that is nonetheless true. The Bible is chock-full of these, and it creates tension. For example, Jesus taught that if we want to live, we must die. If we wish to receive, we must give away. If we want to be free, we must become slaves. The Bible teaches that God is one, and yet, God is three.

Enjoy the paradoxes.

There are lots of spiritual weirdos, so try to study books by writers who stay close to doctrines that have survived for centuries.

Don't Try to Resolve All the Mysteries

Enjoy the mystery. Let's face it: some Bible verses just don't make sense. What, for instance, did Paul mean when he alluded to the Corinthians' baptizing "for the dead"?[29] *What was that?* If we ask and study and ponder and still don't come up with an answer, I think we need to be okay with not figuring it out. All the parts that I don't get, I relegate to the idea that "the secret things belong to the LORD."[30] Faith is supposed to have mystery in it. Paul penned, "Now to him who is able to do immeasurably more than all we ask or imagine . . ."[31]

When you run into principles, analogies, stories, or events in the Bible that are mysterious, smile. Be satisfied with not knowing exactly what is going on. I'm not saying to not try to figure them out, but after you try and still come up empty, chill. Be okay with not being fully omniscient.

Watch Out!

When I drive, I drive suspiciously. I am suspicious that I may crash, so I don't reach cruising speed, put on the cruise control, and read a book. I watch the road. I am suspicious that other drivers may run into me, so I drive defensively. When I read the Bible, I am suspicious that I have biases (some I'm not even aware of), so I try to be humble and watchful.

Christians need to challenge one another's BluBlockers—to question things more; to use common sense; to point out how opinions predispose us to judgments and how prejudice, closed-mindedness, and bigotry invariably produce destructive Blus. For example, I always go to DEFCON 1 whenever I hear a televangelist or Christian friend say, "The Lord showed me that this verse means . . ." and then proceed to tell me something that doesn't stand up against common sense. More often than not, it isn't the Lord at all—it's the person's own destructive set of "I have unique insights" shades.

Let's face it: some Bible verses just don't make sense.

History is full of examples of people using biblical texts to justify the denigration or persecution or disenfranchising of others—all while considering themselves to be true bearers of the uncompromised "Word of God." *Watch out.* Always approach Scripture with the awareness that you are wearing BluBlockers. If you do so, you will have a great shot at keeping out of the land of weirdness and finding the "endurance and the encouragement of the Scriptures"[32] that bring us hope.

09

>>A TORTUROUS HELL

it bothers me that the christian faith includes a hell

The "creep factor" shoots pretty high when you start thinking or talking about hell. Definitely a disturbing topic. It surprised me to discover that God is uncomfortable with the subject too. Scripture suggests that he hates hell, and he hates that people are going there.[1] God's dream is for all to experience eternal life. But the problem still exists: the Bible says there is a hell, and people are going to go there *forever.* I still can't get my mind around that.

Jesus said hell was "the eternal fire prepared for the devil and his angels,"[2] not for human beings. John 3:16, the most famous verse in the Bible, affirms that God's heart aches over the idea that *any* person is going there: "For God so loved the world that he gave his one and only Son, that whoever believes in him *shall not perish* but have eternal life." Peter wrote that God is "not wanting anyone to perish, but everyone to come to repentance."[3]

If God hates the idea so much, why is there a hell? And why does it have to be forever? And why does it have to be a place of absolute horror and abject despair? Again, faith turns out to be less than tidy. I've struggled with these questions and find it troubling that God doesn't answer issues like these directly. I just don't get it.

And yet I am also haunted by the conviction that God is good. I find solace in the notion that—just as there were many things I couldn't explain to my kids as they were growing up—perhaps some matters of eternity are beyond our human capacity to understand. At one point Jesus said, "I have much more to say to you, more than you can now bear."[4] This may not assuage all the anxiety fostered by my questioning mind, but it does help to know my questions will some day be answered. That being said, I keep on scratching and clawing for more insight and understanding. God promised, "Call to me and I will answer you and tell you great and unsearchable things you do not know."[5]

So, what do we know from Scripture on this very difficult topic? Why is there a hell? And what is it like?

Most, if not all, people's concepts of hell are not found in the Bible at all but have bled into Christian thought through writers such as the Italian poet Dante Alighieri (1265–1321), author of *The Divine Comedy,* and the English poet John Milton (1608–1674), author of *Paradise Lost.* One would assume that asking what the Bible teaches about the subject would yield a straightforward answer, but it doesn't turn out that way. In the final analysis, the Bible is somewhat ambiguous on the topic.

A fascinating book, *Four Views on Hell,* edited by William Crockett, features him and three other evangelical systematic theologians debating their conflicting personal beliefs about hell. Each of the four contributors passionately believes that his own interpretation of hell is accurately derived from the biblical text. Four conservative evangelical scholars, four different views of hell. Hmmm.

>>BASICS BELIEFS ABOUT HELL

Before we address two of these views in some detail, let's look at some points about hell that most scholars agree on.

Not Part of the Original Plan

Many people don't realize that hell was never part of God's creation; it was added later because of the appearance of rebellion in his creation. This is important to recognize, because the essence of hell is about relationship. Hell is the result of created beings rejecting a relationship with their Creator. God created hell to provide these God rejecters with the opportunity for relational separation—separation and isolation from him—the place where he *is not.* Hell is the place where the objects of God's love are beyond his ability to love. No wonder God hates this place. Any parent would.

Think of the torment of that place, the place where God is not. Remember, God is the one who is life, the one responsible for all the good we know.[6] A life apart from him would be a life without provision, protection, beauty, friends, family, hope, love, joy—everything that is good or that matters. This would not be life at all; it would be *anti*life. Such is the dimension called hell. Those who dwell there will be void of everything that makes a human, human. They will be, in the words of Peter, "like brute beasts, creatures of instinct."[7] They will be lost to God's goodness forever.

Not Easy to Go to Hell

Many people mistakenly believe that people easily end up in hell. All it takes is one misstep—an unconfessed sin, some spiritual laziness, or a failure to pray the "sinner's prayer." But people are not *sent* to hell, they *go* there. The journey demands that a person reject God by ignoring God's relevance in his or her life, and that doesn't happen all at once. Such rejection is the culmination of thousands of choices (conscious and unconscious) that one makes throughout a lifetime. *It is not easy to go to hell.*

People are not *sent* to hell, they *go* there.

In the final analysis hell is not so much a sentence for doing bad things as much as it is the end of a path someone has committed to throughout life—the path of habitually ignoring or rejecting the relevance of Christ. Our trajectory for eternity is set by the habitual decisions we make in the warp and woof of daily life. If we habitually exercise trust in God, we are preparing ourselves for being with him and his people for eternity. However, if we continually ignore or push off from trusting him in favor of trusting in ourselves, we set a course that keeps us moving away from God. As we slip into eternity our trajectory is set. Either our arc has us moving toward God and heaven, or away from him, which is the path to hell.

Think of an astronaut floating in space. Once he has pushed off from his spacecraft he doesn't stop moving in that direction until he hits the place where that trajectory ends. Heaven or hell becomes the "end of the line" for each of us, depending on which direction our souls were headed when we entered eternal "space."

No Interest in Knowing God

Scripture suggests that the people who end up in hell will show no interest in wanting to be with God as he is revealed in Jesus Christ. It's not that they will want hell; it's that they do not want Jesus Christ. Remember that salvation is not really a gift *from* God as much as it is the gift *of* God. God is the gift, but not all want him. The Bible claims that in the future, when God is actually seen face-to-face, those who ignore or reject him will scramble to find a place to hide from him. Not just because of fear; it's also that they won't want anything to do with him. Speaking of that day, Isaiah declared, "Men will flee to caves in the rocks and to holes in the ground from dread of the LORD and the splendor of his majesty."[8]

It's not that they will want hell; it's that they do not want Jesus Christ.

Think of folks you know who want nothing to do with Jesus Christ. You bring him up in a conversation, and they break into a sweat and quickly either change the subject or head for the door. The longer people live separated from God, the less likely they are to exercise their free will to turn and trust him. (That's why most people who come to Christ come while they are young.) The longer a person lives in a habit, the harder it is to break that habit. If you die while you are in the God-ignoring habit, you will be lost to any desire to make him relevant in your afterlife. The resistance a person has in his or her heart in the *now* will only be intensified *then.*

Have you ever been at the mall or in another public place and seen someone you know who usually makes you feel uncomfortable? What do you do? Most of us try to duck out from being seen. We don't want to face the person. It's too unpleasant. Multiplying that by a billion might get us close to understanding why lifelong God rejecters will try to hide from him in caves and holes in the ground. As you read the sacred text, you get the feeling that the gates of hell will be locked from the inside! A dark, tormenting, isolated hell is the home of choice of those who are terrified of the One they have rejected all their lives. Their God-ignoring, God-rejecting trajectory was set by the way in which they lived their lives.

Renowned theologian D. A. Carson says it well: "Hell is not a place where people are consigned because they were pretty good blokes, but they just didn't believe the right stuff. They're consigned there, first and foremost, because they defy their maker and want to be at the center of the universe. Hell is . . . filled with people who, for all eternity, *still* want to be the center of the universe and who persist in their God-defying rebellion."[9]

A Matter of Choice

What most miss is that the creation of hell is actually a sign of how much God values the human will. Remember, God's will—his great longing—is that no one perish, not a single person. So why does he allow anyone to do so? Because he created human beings with free will, and he has no intention of violating that. We are not modified monkeys, subject to instinct alone; we are unique creatures who have the power to cognate, reason, and choose. God will not force his purpose on us (though the purpose he set for the human race is one that causes us to flourish in a way nothing else can!). We can choose to reject God's purpose for us (and to ignore or reject God). God created us with that right. Sadly, many do choose to ignore and reject God. This is the worm that has curled its way into the apple of the human condition.

Here's the deal: we humans either have free will or we don't. If we do, then God cannot strip us of the right to choose, even if we choose something he did not want for us. That means it would be a violation of our free will for God to force us to be with him for eternity if we don't want to be. By allowing us to say no to him, God is actually showing respect for us and keeping human dignity intact.

It would be a violation of our free will for God to force us to be with him for eternity.

Father Dermot A. Lane wrote, "Hell is not God's creation. It is not the outcome of some additional divine sentence for punishment or retribution. Nor is it 'a place' to which God 'sends' sinners. Instead hell is a freely chosen final destiny, involving the punishment and suffering that results from a persistent lifestyle of self-isolation in deliberate and conscious opposition to God."[10]

The formation of hell is not an indication that God is mean, angry, or capricious—like a spoiled child who is hacked off about not getting his own way—so he decides to make the disobedient pay. It is evidence that God will never force himself on the human race. It evidences that he honors human will by choosing to create a place where *he is not.*

Some wonder since God is grieved by the necessity of hell, why doesn't he just force everyone into heaven (or maybe they could just go to hell for a while)? This seems more congruent with love. The problem is this position does not reflect the Bible, but our modern American sentimentalism. We believe love and tenderness mitigate harsher virtues such as justice and righteousness. However, true love would never force people into heaven, even if it were for their own good. Such an action would actually be immoral, because it would mean that God only uses people as a means to an end—to get what *he* wants. Working against a person's will is coercion, not love. When you force people to do something against their free will, you dehumanize them.

I believe that one of the reasons God obscures his presence is because he refuses to violate our free will. Think of what would happen if God appeared in his power and glory at different times in people's lives. They would be intimidated. His opaqueness affords people the space to do what *they* would like to do without intimidation. People often act differently when they are being watched. God chooses to maintain a delicate balance between making himself known and hiding his presence so that people who want to ignore him can do so freely. Though it causes him much pain when people choose to reject him, it also makes it all the sweeter when people freely choose to follow him.

God chooses to maintain a delicate balance between making himself known and hiding his presence so that people who want to ignore him can do so freely.

How About a Second Chance?

Some Christ followers reason along this line: If God really loves people and wants everyone to be saved, why doesn't he give people a second chance, after death, to make the decision to follow him? Surely people would run to God once they experienced the horror of hell for a minute or two—why not give them another shot?

Again, this is an example of good ole' American sentimentality falling short as it tries to work out deeply complex theological-ethical issues. The very question carries with it the assumption that God did not do everything he could have done for that person to make the right choice the first time around. It's a wrong assumption.

The Bible claims the main reason for the delay in Jesus' return has to do with his longing for people to have as much time and space as they need in order to change. Peter wrote, "God isn't late with his promise as some measure lateness. He is restraining himself on account of you, holding back the End because he doesn't want anyone lost. He's giving everyone space and time to change."[11] From verses like these, one could surmise that God may actually delay the deaths of people until they have had time to make a choice about eternity. If this turns out to be the case, no one will be able to accuse God of not giving him enough time to get his life right with God.

God is fair and just. So what about those people who have never heard the gospel message? Will they go to hell too? Scripture tells us God has made a way for every person to be judged on the basis of the knowledge that individual does have. Paul wrote:

> When outsiders who have never heard of God's law follow it more or less by instinct, they confirm its truth by their obedience. They show that God's law is not something alien, imposed on us from without, but woven into the very fabric of our creation. There is something deep within them that echoes God's yes and no, right and wrong. Their response to God's yes and no will become public knowledge on the day God makes his final decision about every man and woman. The Message from God that I proclaim through Jesus Christ takes into account all these differences.[12]

If God were to allow a second chance after death, then life before death would be irrelevant. If the decision about being a God follower could be made later, in eternity, who would care how they lived on this planet? But life on this planet does matter. Scripture asserts, "Each person is destined to die once and after that comes judgment."[13] Life on Earth is all about making a choice. After this life, choice is no longer an option. Joshua captured the heart of the matter when he told the Israelites, "Choose for yourselves this day whom you will serve . . . as for me and my household, we will serve the LORD."[14]

If God were to allow a second chance after death, then life before death would be irrelevant.

We make our choices *here* in *this life*. There are no second chances.

Why Not Annihilate Hell's Inhabitants?

Some wonder why God doesn't simply annihilate those who don't make it to heaven. On some level snuffing out those who are banished to hell seems more humane than letting them suffer in agony forever. Some theologians believe this will be the case—that people who go to hell will be ultimately annihilated.

But I disagree, because allowing people to be forever separated from God is morally superior to annihilating them. Why? Because annihilating them would mean God is making the judgment, "If you don't follow me, you have no right to exist, even in death." It would say that people should be terminated because they are of no further use to God, that people only have *instrumental* value to him. This would signify that people only have worth for what they do *for* God—a kind of means to an end, instead of being valuable just because they exist. The truth is, God thinks everyone has intrinsic value, independent of the choices they make, whether or not he approves of those choices. God is the sustainer of persons.

Perhaps the strongest argument against annihilation is that only one kind of being has both an eternal and physical dimension—we human beings. We are a spirit-soul-body creation.[15] The spirit part of us is eternal—that part is like indestructible asbestos; it can never die. That means annihilation is not even a possibility. If God had planned on exterminating humans, he would never have put that eternal component into us.

>>TWO PROMINENT VIEWS

Now let's look at the two most common views conservative evangelicals have about hell, and let's try to answer the question of what hell will be like.

The Literal View

Historically, the church has taken the biblical texts about hell literally. This view maintains that the flames are literal, as are the burning brimstone, smoke, flesh-eating worms, and unquenchable thirst. On this view, a righteous God is merely doling out justice to the wicked by requiring them to endure these everlasting and terrible tortures. The unimaginably tormented will be aware that they will never have relief from their endless punishment, which will only serve to add greatly to their suffering. Creepy indeed.

To no one's surprise, this view has garnered some critics. Atheist Richard Dawkins said, "Who will say with confidence that sexual abuse is more permanently damaging to children than threatening them with the eternal and unquenchable fires of hell?"[16] Charles Templeton said, "I couldn't hold someone's hand to a fire for a moment. Not an instant! How could a loving God, just because you don't obey him and do what he wants, torture you forever—not allowing you to die, but to continue in that pain for eternity? There is no *criminal* who would do this!"[17]

Perhaps the untenable notion of everlasting torment is why we hear so few sermons on hell. If one takes the literal view, silence appears to be the watchword (if only because of the general embarrassment many Christians feel about the subject). Yet, according to Scripture, a grim fate awaits those who choose to ignore or reject the relevance of Jesus Christ.

The Metaphorical View

However, not all Christians embrace the belief that hell is going to be a literal burning abyss where unimagined torment is meted out to lost souls throughout eternity. Many evangelical scholars say that careful exegesis of the Bible does not support the literal view, but that many of the expressions describing hell are figurative in nature. Even John Calvin determined that the "eternal fire" in texts like Matthew 3:12 is better understood metaphorically.[18]

William Crockett writes, "From my own informal survey, I would guess that most evangelicals interpret hell's fires metaphorically, or at least allow for the possibility that hell might be something other than literal fire."[19] His "survey" involved well-known, cautious evangelicals the likes of F. F. Bruce, Billy Graham, C. S. Lewis, and J. I. Packer.

On this view, hell is a dimension where the unsaved will spend eternity in torment and agony, but the extreme pain and environmental conditions described in the Bible are not interpreted literally, which means hell is not primarily a torture chamber. The biblical descriptions of heat, bondage, darkness, thirst, worms, pain, flogging, and fire are taken as symbols of the emotional and psychological pain of being separated from God (who is life) and from relationships with all other people. Imagine the horror of being in outer darkness, launched out into space with no one else around forever and ever and ever. There is no end. No turning back. Alone . . . forever. Even the pagan philosopher Aristotle acknowledged that sharing our lives with others is critical for a healthy life. He said that if "each man lives as he pleases," he lives "as the Cyclopes do."[20] The mythical Cyclopes were mean, destructive beings, with a single eye—only for themselves.

The idea of judgment has always been simple: Initially, God brings it to bear in this life, in order to help us change our ill-gotten habits. If we persistently say no to him, in spite of initial judgment, he eventually leaves us alone. That is final judgment—God backing out of our lives. Final judgment is the result of our lifelong refusal to submit to the person of Jesus, to his help and love. When we ignore or reject Jesus, we ignore or reject God himself, along with all his freedom and forgiveness. Final judgment is the absence of freedom and forgiveness and only comes when we refuse God's mercy. Scripture says, "Did you think that because he's such a nice God, he'd let you off the hook? Better think this one through from the beginning. God is kind, but he's not soft. In kindness he takes us firmly by the hand and leads us into a radical life-change. You're

Final judgment is the absence of freedom and forgiveness and only comes when we refuse God's mercy.

not getting by with anything. Every refusal and avoidance of God adds fuel to the fire. The day is coming when it's going to blaze hot and high, God's fiery and righteous judgment."[21]

Ultimately, the point of hell is to allow people to continue the pattern of living they embraced while on earth. Some practiced life without acknowledging or submitting to God. The problem, as they will soon discover, is that all the good they knew on this earth, which came from God, will disappear in his absence; there will be nothing good left. Even their capacity to feel good things like love, joy, peace, and a sense of purpose will be gone because even the capacity for goodness comes from God. Hell is the place where God is not; where *good* is not; where feelings of impatience, dread, fear, hopelessness, self-pity, and anger prevail. It is the place of *un*good. Though not an official chamber of torture, it will be a place of punishment and deep darkness.

>>METAPHORICAL IMAGES

As we've seen, the Bible gives us some shocking images about hell. Should we take those images literally, or should we see them as metaphors pointing to a real but indefinable state? No one is fighting for a metaphorical view in an attempt to brush off the harsh teaching about hell in the Bible. If the images of hell are to be taken literally, then we should accept those images at face value. After all, Christians say they believe what the Bible teaches. We should not adopt a softer view simply because it violates our American sensibilities to do so. We cannot allow sentimentality to dull or undermine the authority of Scripture. But there are some compelling reasons why scholars do not take the descriptions of fire and worms literally.

As we saw in the chapter on negotiating Scripture, a number of texts in the Bible are obviously not to be taken literally. When a text is seen as metaphorical, the meanings are actually richer and deeper than if they were interpreted literally. For example, when Jesus says, "If anyone comes to me and does not hate his father and mother, his wife and children, his brothers and sisters . . . he cannot be my disciple,"[22] he is not saying we must actually "hate" our families to be his followers. He is using metaphorical language to communicate the idea that loyalty to him must be supreme in a disciple's life. In addition, when he said, "If your right eye causes you to sin, gouge it out and throw it away,"[23] we know he did not mean this literally, because the context was dealing with cutting off lust. Tearing out your physical eyes can't stop lust; blind people lust too.

When examining the descriptions of hell (or heaven, for that matter), we find the imagery a little confusing. For instance, the text says there is no need for the sun or moon to shine in heaven, for the radiance of God will fill the city.[24] What does that mean? And when the city is actually described, it is unlike anything ever seen before. Are the words to be taken literally, or is the message that heaven is beyond our wildest dreams? Perhaps it is, as Paul intimated, a place "No eye has seen, no ear has heard, no mind has conceived."[25]

The literal view of hell has produced some of the wildest *extra*biblical writings one could imagine. In the fourteenth century, Dante "imagined a place of absolute terror where the damned writhe and scream, while the blessed bask in the glory of Eternal Light. The descriptions of hell come complete with loud wails of sinners boiling in blood, terrified and naked people running from hordes of biting snakes, and lands of heavy darkness and dense fog. In Dante's hell, people must endure thick, burning smoke that chars their nostrils, and some remain forever trapped in lead cloaks, a claustrophobic nightmare."[26]

American theologian Jonathan Edwards ran with the idea that hell was literally a furnace of fire:

> The body will be full of torment as full as it can hold, and every part of it shall be full of torment. They shall be in extreme pain, every joint of 'em, every never shall be full of inexpressible torment. They shall be tormented even to their fingers' ends. The whole body shall be full of the wrath of God. Their hearts and their bowels and their heads, their eyes and their tongues, their hands and their feet will be filled with the fierceness of God's wrath. This is taught us in many Scriptures.[27]

Descriptions like Dante's and Edwards' have proven somewhat effective at jolting folks to repentance, but the Scriptures do not explicitly teach what these men imagined. Certainly, the Bible teaches that hell will be a place of frightful judgment, but precisely what it will be like physically is questionable.

Let's talk about "fire" first. In an interview with journalist Lee Strobel, conservative evangelical scholar J. P. Moreland points out, "We know that the reference to flames is figurative because if you try to take it literally, it makes no sense. For example, hell is described as a place of utter darkness and yet there are flames, too. How can that be? Flames would light things up."[28]

But there is more. The flame imagery speaks beyond literal fire. Fire has been symbolic of judgment all through the Scriptures. For example, we are told Christ is going to return surrounded by flames.[29] It also says he will have a big sword coming out of his mouth when he returns.[30] Nobody thinks Christ is performing a literal circus sword-swallowing trick here. The flames and sword stand for Christ coming in judgment. Fire is used in another verse to describe God as a "consuming fire."[31] Nobody thinks he is actually a gigantic, cosmic Bunsen burner. Again, the flame imagery is a way of talking about judgment. We are not diminishing these texts by looking at them metaphorically—in fact, they come alive as we do! We must interpret the fire of hell as a portrait that symbolizes the wrath and judgment of God. The words are not necessarily indicating a literal, fiery abyss, but a severe (though unspecified) judgment that awaits those who are God ignorers.

Nobody thinks God is actually a gigantic, cosmic Bunsen burner.

What about the "worms" Jesus mentions that will eat people's flesh in hell? Will they be in hell? In Jesus' day there was a sewage area into which the blood and fat of thousands of animals from the weekly sacrifices held in the temple would flow. Worms constantly ingested that stuff where it pooled just outside the city gate. Jesus referred to that wormy place, calling it "hell." But did he really mean that hell was going to be the sewage pit outside of Jerusalem's gate? Or did he mean that hell was going to be worse than that disgusting, odorous, abandoned place? Everyone present would have understood he was speaking metaphorically and not literally.

Then there's the phrase "gnashing of teeth."[32] You can take it literally as the reaction to physical torment, or you can take it as an expression of rage. Ever see how self-centered, self-absorbed, highly narcissistic two-year-olds grind their teeth and growl in anger when they don't get their own way? Perhaps "gnashing of teeth" symbolizes the anger that will be realized as hell dwellers discover their deep, permanent loss of all that is good.

If there are no literal flames or worms or gnashing of teeth, does that mean hell isn't such a bad place after all? Nothing could be further from the truth! Back to Moreland: "It would be a mistake to think that [hell isn't that bad]. Any figure of speech has a literal point. What is figurative is the burning flame; what is literal is that this is a place of utter heartbreak. It is a loss of everything, and it's meant to stand for the fact that hell is the worst possible situation that could ever happen to a person."[33]

Hell avoidance is not to be used as a foundation for faith.

Though the doctrine of hell is scary enough to be spiritually motivating, hell avoidance is not to be used as a foundation for faith. John wrote, "We love [God] because he first loved us."[34] He didn't say, "We love God because we're all afraid of going to hell."

>>AN ALTERNATIVE VISION OF REALITY

It seems to me that Jesus and the early church were more concerned about creating a community of people who lived differently than they were about getting ready for eternity. They believed something unique. They believed that the events of Jesus' life, death, and resurrection—and the story that those events carry forward into the present—really do make sense of life. These men and women aligned themselves with that story, which made them different—they belonged to Jesus

Christ, who was present to live in and through them. They had an alternative vision of reality, a vision that demanded a nonconformist value system. This alternative vision was different from the one heralded by the religious and political contexts they found themselves in. These Christ followers testified to the life, death, resurrection, and ascension of Jesus Christ by their willingness to die, if need be, in order to fulfill the *missio dei* (the mission of God) in the world.

But today, relatively few think of Christianity as a call to enter a new kind of living—a life jacked up with adventure, mission, and divine destiny. Faith for many is nothing more than fire insurance from hell—an acquiescence to rule keeping (it's the least we can do) and a safety net of forgiveness when we break the rules. I find that disturbing. On this view the human experience of faith isn't much more than a life of stumbling and bumbling around, holding on to faith the best we can till Christ sees fit to bring us home.

Faith for many is nothing more than fire insurance from hell.

But what if the Christian life is supposed to be more than that? What if it is a calling for us to step into something larger than ourselves? What if God is inviting us into something more than hell avoidance? What if he is inviting us to participate in some kind of *divine quest*?

In J. R. R. Tolkien's classic *The Hobbit*, Bilbo Baggins lives contentedly in his home at Bag End, Hobbiton, until one spring morning the wizard Gandalf visits him. Gandalf, sensing that there was a hunger for adventure beating secretly in Bilbo's heart, said to him, "There is more to you than you know."

Bilbo, it turns out, was part of the Took clan, on his mother's side. They were the ancient defenders of the Shire. Gandalf knew that—though Bilbo may have inherited the easygoing nature of the Hobbits from his father's side—his Tookish thirst for adventure would eventually lead him to go beyond the safety of the Shire into the adventure that would save the world.

I think God put something "Tookish" in all of us. Erwin McManus writes, "There was a voice screaming inside my head, *Don't sleep through your dreams!* Ever heard that voice? It calls you like a temptress to abandon the monotony of life and to begin an adventure. It threatens to leave you in the mundane if you refuse to risk all that you have for all that could be."[35]

"There was a voice screaming inside my head, *Don't sleep through your dreams!*"

Something in us wants to be part of saving the world. True, we inherited things from Adam that make us cower and lunge into survival and protection mode; we also have a drive that wants to make a difference, that wants to glorify God. We don't have to settle for being hell-avoiding legalists who only color inside the lines, or reward-seeking saints who are so heavenly minded they are of little earthly good. Instead, we can be spiritual pioneers—adventurers who dare to explore what a life fully committed to God can really look like.

>>DARE TO IMAGINE MORE

Imagine if Christians started running at making this a better world: A world that is "filled with the knowledge of the glory of the LORD, as the waters cover the sea."[36] A world where the church is "salt" and "light,"[37] which means we make life a little tastier for people; it means our presence eliminates rot and dispels darkness.

A world where believers fearlessly contend against evil and make no peace with oppression. A world where the church consistently uses its freedom to maintain justice in our communities and among the nations. A world where believers imagine themselves to be (as our Savior Jesus was) people who come not to be served but to serve. And by following in Jesus' steps, we have the wisdom, patience, and courage to minister to the suffering, the friendless, and the needy in his name. *Imagine that.*

Imagine if we started to believe in the power of prayer. What could happen then? Jesus said, "Therefore I tell you, whatever you ask for in prayer, believe that you have received it, and it will be yours."[38] Maybe Jesus was daring us to "believe" that when we pray about a matter, God will address it.

That would mean we could pray for world peace and actually expect something to happen. We could ask God to "Kindle in every heart the true love of peace, and guide with your wisdom those who take counsel for the nations of the earth, that in tranquility your dominion may increase until the earth is filled with the knowledge of your love; through Jesus Christ our Lord."[39] *Imagine that.*

Imagine a world free from hunger and prejudice; a world where we see the fulfillment of God's promise, "I will pour out my Spirit on all people."[40] Imagine the nations coming to God in worldwide renewal in fulfillment of the promise in the Psalms: "Ask of me, and I will make the nations your inheritance, the ends of the earth your possession."[41] What if we asked and actually expected an answer?

What if Paul wasn't kidding when he declared, "Now to him who is able to do immeasurably more than all we ask *or imagine.*"[42] What if we dared to imagine more? The Bible promises that a day is coming when "the dwelling of God" will be with people, "and he will live with them." It claims that we "will be his people, and God himself will be with them and be their God." It promises: "He will wipe every tear from their eyes. There will be no more death or mourning or crying or pain, for the old order of things has passed away."[43]

What if we imagined a world where God always dwells with us and where all tears are wiped away and where all crying and pain are gone? What if we are to carry *that* vision in our minds? Theologians tell us that there is an eschatological tension in the kingdom of God—that in one sense the kingdom of God is *here*, but in another sense, *not yet*. Jesus told us, "The kingdom of God is at hand," and yet spoke of it as coming in the future. It's on a continuum somewhere between "here" and "not yet." And apparently believers have something to do with where it is. Jesus told Christians to pray to the Father, asking, "Thy kingdom come, thy will be done *in earth, as it is in heaven.*"[44]

In one sense the kingdom of God is *here*, but in another sense, *not yet*.

However much of the kingdom we can experience here on this earth, we know we will never fully experience it until Jesus returns. But the kingdom *is* among us in some measure, and we can experience it *now*, at least like the measles—in spots. What if we Christ followers used our faith to attract more of the kingdom into our here and now?

If Christians did this, then when they encountered the tears and crying and pain so present in this fallen world, they would move toward it, bringing with them the hope of the eternal vision. Isn't that what the church is supposed to be?

Perhaps this is what the writer of Hebrews was referring to when he wrote that the follower of Jesus could partake of "the powers of the coming age."[45] It is with these thoughts in mind that the *Book of Common Prayer* leads us to pray, "Give to us the peace and unity of that heavenly City."[46]

Dude. Those are some sweet imaginings.

>>FINAL THOUGHTS

to believe or not to believe

Jesus once preached a message so disturbing it caused thousands to turn from following him. The narrative reads, "After this a lot of his disciples left. They no longer wanted to be associated with him." Immediately after this happened, Jesus turned to the twelve apostles and gave them a chance to do the same: "Do you also want to leave?" he asked. Peter replied, "Master, to whom would we go? You have the words of real life, eternal life. We've already committed ourselves, confident that you are the Holy One of God."[1]

I agree with Peter.

We may not like it, but the nature of faith makes it an untidy enterprise. It demands persistence in the face of uncertainty. Real faith has doubt in the mix, as the coin has two sides.

What if Jesus *isn't* the answer? What if he is the question?

This makes many Christ followers nervous. They view qualms and questions as evidence of a lack of faith and insist, "Jesus is the answer!" But what if Jesus *isn't* the answer? What if he is the *question*? What if we aren't supposed to have all the answers? Could it be that in the discomfort of unanswered questions we are forced to face our own pride and admit we only "know in part"?[2] Is it possible that questions cause us to face the choice to believe or not to believe?

There is a great story in the life of Jesus where he asked a man if he had faith. The man responded, "I do believe; help me overcome my unbelief!"[3] Notice that it is possible to believe and still be wrestling with "unbelief." Just because you have misgivings does not mean you do not have faith. The guy in the Jesus story asked that his doubt be "overcome" so that it would not be the prevailing force in his life.

I believe God wants people of faith to question, to be bothered, to seek for tenable answers, to consider the "What if it's true?" juxtaposed against the "What if it's not true?" Faith is not the result of quelling all doubt but the result of a choice after one has earnestly sought to understand. It is a venture of human consideration and divine illumination. It's hard, sometimes painful, often disorienting, and always messy—certainly not a cheery, no-conflict, refreshingly bubbly, perpetually happy place. Only in a world where faith is difficult can faith exist.

If this is a true description of faith, then faith is more like an intense mud-wrestling contest than anything else. Our role is to stay in the ring, even though we don't see God all that clearly and even though it would be easier to quit than to stay in the fray. When we hang in there, fighting through uncertainty and doubt, we are living by faith.

When I look at the Bible and Christian faith, I am left with some formidable, disturbing questions. And I don't have the answers. I may never have them this side of eternity. I hate that, but it is what it is. In spite of what bothers me about faith, I choose to be a God follower, and because I am, he meets me where I am, despite my questions. And that is worth it all!

I read a quote from notable scholar and author Dallas Willard that captures the why behind my decision to forever follow Jesus: "The issue is, what do we want? The Bible says that if you seek God with all your heart, then you will surely find him. *Surely* find him. It's the person who wants to know God that God reveals himself to. And if a person doesn't want to know God—well, God has created the world and the human mind in such a way that he doesn't have to."[4]

I have found him. And I don't want out.

>>ACKNOWLEDGMENTS

Writing doesn't come easy for me. It's a bit like painting a house with a paint-by-numbers paintbrush—lots of painstaking work. In this particular book I found myself frequently caught between the borders of skepticism and belief, confusion and clarity, and mystery and resolve. I often felt like I was a man without a country. A number of wonderful people helped me sort out my thoughts and helped me clarify my "voice" in this writing: my wonderful colleagues Andrew Arndt and Kathy Law, and the mentor and architect of my writing career, Tina Jacobson. Thank you.

The really hard work fell to my brilliant, tough-minded editor, Liz Heaney, and my publisher and kind friend, Philis Boultinghouse, who did the most to help me reshape the book through several iterations until it became something that was actually readable. They definitely made me sound better than I really am. Thanks, girls!

I am also deeply grateful to the members and staff of Sanctuary (www.sanctuarytulsa.com), the community of faith where I serve as lead pastor. Those wonderful folks continue to afford me the gift of time, so I can sit for days and days at a time—away from the daily responsibilities of pastoral care—in order to write. Thank you, thank you, thank you.

It turns out that books, like children, are raised by the efforts of a village.

>>ENDNOTES

>>chapter 01

1 Isaiah 45:15
2 Isaiah 45:15
3 Luke 24:16
4 Genesis 28:16
5 Deuteronomy 31:18
6 See Psalms 10:1, 13:1, 89:46
7 Matthew 11:25
8 Luke 18:34
9 Luke 19:42
10 Matthew 13:13
11 1 Corinthians 2:7
12 Ephesians 3:9
13 Colossians 1:26, WEB
14 1 Timothy 2:4
15 See Colossians 1:17
16 See Acts 17:26
17 See Acts 14:17
18 Acts 17:25
19 Isaiah 55:6

20 1 Chronicles 16:11
21 Jeremiah 29:14
22 Matthew 7:7
23 Ephesians 5:32
24 James 4:8
25 Romans 1:19–20
26 Romans 2:15
27 Romans 10:20
28 Acts 17:22
29 Acts 17:26
30 Acts 17:23, MSG
31 Acts 17:27
32 Acts 17:28
33 Richard Dawkins, *The God Delusion* (Boston: Houghton Mifflin, 2006), 168.
34 Ecclesiastes 3:11
35 See Romans 1:18–32
36 2 Thessalonians 3:2
37 Matthew 11:17
38 Blaise Pascal, *Pensées*, trans. A. J. Krailsheimer, rev. ed, 1966, repr. (London: Penguin Books, 1995), 50.
39 John 12:28–29
40 Luke 18:8
41 Genesis 6:5
42 Romans 1:19
43 See Matthew 11:25
44 Matthew 18:3
45 Romans 1:20
46 Romans 1:21
47 Matthew 5:3–9

48 Matthew 5:8
49 1 Peter 5:5
50 1 Corinthians 1:21, TLB
51 1 Corinthians 1:19
52 1 Corinthians 1:27
53 Revelation 6:16
54 John 6:44–46
55 Matthew 5:6
56 Jeremiah 29:13
57 Matthew 12:38–39
58 Luke 23:8
59 See Matthew 27:49
60 Luke 16:28–31
61 John 12:37–40
62 Romans 1:18–21
63 Romans 1:22–24

>>chapter 02

1 Michael Shermer, *How We Believe: Science, Skepticism, and the Search for God* (New York: Freeman, 2000), 16–31.
2 Hebrews 11:1
3 Matthew 11:25, TLB
4 2 Thessalonians 3:2
5 Ephesians 2:8
6 Romans 10:17, emphasis added
7 Revelation 3:20
8 See Psalm 139:16; Acts 17:26
9 Exodus 33:15
10 Psalm 63:8, AMP

11 Galatians 2:20

12 Matthew 7:7

13 1 John 4:19

14 Ephesians 3:20

15 Romans 11:33

16 Anselm, *The Major Works* Trans: Brian Davies, Gillian Rosemary Evans (Oxford: Oxford University Press, 1998), 87.

>>chapter 03

1 Peter Maas, "Top Ten War Crimes Suspects," *George*, June 1999, 53.

2 Peter Kreeft, *Making Sense Out of Suffering* (Ann Arbor, MI: Servant: 1986), viii.

3 The Omni Poll, Barna Research Group, Ltd., January 1999, quoted in Lee Strobel, *The Case for Faith* (Grand Rapids, Zondervan, 2000), 29.

4 D. A. Carson, *How Long, O Lord: Reflections on Suffering and Evil* (Ada, MI: Baker Academic, 2 Edition, 2006), 17–18.

5 Matthew 6:10, KJV, emphasis added

6 Matthew 6:13, KJV

7 1 John 5:4

8 1 John 5:18

9 Job 1:1

10 Job 34:11

11 Romans 8:28

12 Adapted from *Pain: The Gift That Nobody Wants* by Dr. Paul Brand and Phillip Yancy (Darby, PA: Diane Publishing Co., 1999), pp. 6–7.

13 2 Peter 1:4

14 Genesis 1:10
15 Genesis 1:2, KJV
16 Genesis 1:3
17 Genesis 1:31
18 3 John 11
19 James 1:17
20 Romans 5:18–19, MSG
21 See Ezekiel 28:15
22 See Psalm 147:16
23 See Acts 12:23
24 See Luke 13:4
25 Romans 8:22
26 Jay Livingston and Ray Evans, "Que Será Será" (whatever will be, will be), Jay Livingston Music Inc. & St. Angelo Music, Inc. Published in 1956.
27 Acts 5:38–39, MSG
28 Ephesians 1:11, AMP
29 Romans 9:20, MSG
30 Mark 5:30
31 2 Thessalonians 1:11
32 1 John 5:4
33 2 Chronicles 20:17
34 Exodus 14:13, 15
35 See Hebrews 9:27
36 See Proverbs 3:1–2
37 See Isaiah 38:5
38 See Philippians 1:22
39 Romans 8:28
40 See Revelation 21:1–4
41 Matthew 10:29–31, NLT

42 Catherine Marshall, *Something More* (New York: Inspiration Press, 1990), 191.

43 1 Corinthians 15:26

44 Hembree, Charles, *Pocket of Pebbles* (Grand Rapids: Baker, 1969), 33.

45 See John 16:33

46 Romans 12:21

47 Matthew 5:16, NIV

48 Matthew 25:31–40, MSG

49 Carol Hymowitz, Reporter, "Executives Teach Inmates How to be Employees," *Wall Street Journal*, Monday, March 17, 2008, B1, B3.

50 Revelation 21:1–4

>>chapter 04

1 See John 14:6

2 http://cnn.com/Transcripts/0001/12/lkl.00.html.

3 John 14:6

4 Ravi Zacharias, *Can Man Live Without God* (Nashville: Word, 1994), from introduction by Charles Colson, ix.

5 www.news-release.uiowa.edu/2002/december/1209finding-god.html.

6 http://cnn.com/Transcripts/0001/12/lkl.00html.

7 www.thinkexist.com/swami_vivekenanda/2.html.

8 Richard Wurmbrand, *Tortured for Christ*, (Bartlesville, OK: Living Sacrifice, 1967), 18–19.

9 Romans 2:14–16, MSG

10 Tony Campolo, *Speaking My Mind* (Nashville: W. Publishing, 2004), 151.

11 Acts 17:16
12 Acts 17:23, MSG
13 Acts 17:26
14 Acts 17:27
15 Acts 17:28
16 Acts 14:11
17 Acts 14:17
18 Acts 17:30
19 John 17:3
20 Acts 17:28
21 Acts 17:27
22 Ravi Zacharias, interview with Lee Strobel, quoted in Strobel, *Case for Faith,* 150.
23 2 John 3
24 http://en.wikiquote.org/wiki/Mahatma_Gandhi.
25 http://michellegalo.com/quotes.html.
26 John 6:45
27 See Ephesians 2:8
28 Romans 11:36
29 Zacharias interview, Strobel, *Case for Faith,* 150–51.
30 Zacharias interview, Strobel, *Case for Faith,* 154.
31 John 8:32
32 Hebrews 4:12
33 John 14:9
34 Hebrews 1:3
35 N. T. Wright and Marcus J. Borg, *The Meaning of Jesus* (New York: HarperCollins Publishers, 2007), 157.
36 John 15:19–20, NLT

>>chapter 05

1 Romans 1:20

2 Prometheus was the mythical Greek god known for his wily intelligence, who stole fire from Zeus and gave it to mortals for their use—thus liberating them.

3 Alister McGrath, *The Twilight of Atheism: The Rise and Fall of Disbelief in the Modern World.* (New York: Doubleday, 2004), 83.

4 Twilight, 88

5 Twilight, 87

6 Genesis 1:24

7 Candace Adams, "Leading Nanoscientist Builds Big Faith," *Baptist Standard,* March 15, 2000.

8 Bill Bryson, *A Short History of Nearly Everything* (New York: Broadway Books, 2003), 7.

9 Walter Bradley, interview with Lee Strobel, quoted in Strobel, *Case for Faith,* 103.

10 Carl Sagan, *Broca's Brain* (New York: Random House, 1979), 275.

11 Christopher Hitchens, *God Is Not Great: How Religion Poisons Everything* (New York: Twelve, 2007), 84–85.

12 Bradley interview. Strobel, *Case for Faith,* 101.

13 Charles B. Thaxton, Walter L. Bradley, and Roger L. Olson, *The Mystery of Life's Origin* (Dallas: Lewis and Stanley, 1984), 194.

14 Genesis 1:26

15 http://www.msnbc.com/id/22186054/, accessed November 26, 2008.

16 David E. Roberts, *Existentialism and Religious Belief,* ed. Roger Hazelton (New York: Oxford University Press, 1959), 39.

17 See Proverbs 12:15

18 Peter B. Medawar, *The Limits of Science* (Oxford: Oxford University Press, 1985), 66.

19 Stephen Jay Gould, "Impeaching a Self-Appointed Judge," *Scientific American* 267, no. 1 (1992): 118–21.

20 See Colossians 1:17

21 Isaiah 40:22

22 Carl Sagan, *Cosmos* (New York: Random House, 1980), 4.

23 Earnest Nagel, "Naturalism Reconsidered," in Houston Peterson, ed., *Essays in Philosophy* (New York: Pocket Books, 1960), 490.

>>chapter 06

1 St. Augustine

2 Genesis 1:27

3 Ephesians 5:1

4 Exodus 7:1

5 John 14:9

6 John 14:12

7 John 17:18

8 Eugene H. Peterson, *The Message* (Colorado Springs: NavPress, 2002), 1641.

9 Ken Schei, "What Is an Atheist for Jesus?" www.atheists-for-Jesus.com/about.php.

10 Matthew 7:21–23

11 Acts 9:2

12 Patrick Glynn, *God: The Evidence* (Rocklin, CA: Forum, 1997), 157.

13 Lucian, *The Death of Peregrine,* www.sacred-texts.com/cla/lus/w14/w1420.htm.

14 John 18:36

15 David Chidester, *Christianity: A Global History* (San Francisco: HarperCollins, 2000), 179.

16 Paul Johnson, *A History of Christianity* (New York: Simon and Schuster, 1976), 116–17.

17 O. Friedrich, *The End of the World: A History* (New York: Coward, McCann & Geoghegan, 1982), 74.

18 Friedrich, *End of the World,* 96.

19 C. Mackay, *Extraordinary Popular Delusions and the Madness of Crowds* (1841; reprint, New York: Barnes & Noble, 1993), 78.

20 Matthew 4:8–9

21 John 6:15

22 Isaiah 40:15, 17

23 John 6:15

24 See Matthew 26:52

25 See Luke 9:51–56

26 See Matthew 16:12

27 1 Peter 2:21

28 See Romans 5:10

29 See Luke 10:30–35

30 Erwin Raphael McManus, *Chasing Daylight* (Nashville: Nelson, 2002), 5.

>>chapter 07

1 Thomas Paine, *Age of Reason*, Part 1 (First printed 1794, reprinted by Freethought Press, New York, 1954), 18–19.

2 George H. Smith, *Atheism: The Case Against God* (Amherst, N.Y.: Prometheus, 1989), 76.

3 Exodus 15:3, KJV
4 Genesis 6:5
5 See Genesis 8:21
6 Deuteronomy 18:20
7 Leviticus 20:10
8 Exodus 21:15, 17
9 Leviticus 24:19–20
10 See Genesis 7:23; 38:10; Leviticus 10:2
11 Deuteronomy 7:1–2
12 1 John 4:8
13 Ezekiel 22:29, 31
14 Ezekiel 22:30
15 See Exodus 32
16 See Genesis 18
17 See Isaiah 38:5
18 Jonah 1:1–3, MSG
19 Jonah 3:4–5, MSG
20 Jonah 3:6–9, MSG
21 Jonah 3:10, MSG
22 Jonah 4:1–5, MSG
23 Matthew 19:7–9, MSG
24 See Malachi 2:16
25 Hebrews 1:1, AMP
26 Hebrews 1:2–3, AMP
27 John 14:9
28 Leviticus 24:19–20
29 Matthew 5:38–45
30 See Ephesians 2:1; 1 John 5:19
31 Matthew 3:10
32 John 3:3

33 Ezekiel 36:26–28, MSG

34 John 8:11, KJV

35 See James 1:21, KJV

36 Ephesians 6:12, NLT

37 See Ephesians 2:1–2

38 Romans 12:21

39 Catherine Marshall, *Something More*, (New York: Inspirational Press, 1974), 229–30.

40 2 Peter 2:12

41 1 Timothy 1:9, NLT

42 Romans 13:1–5, NLT

43 Adapted from: http://en.wikipedia.org/wiki/Just_war.

44 Romans 5:5

>>chapter 08

1 Matthew 24:15

2 Philipians 2:14

3 Leviticus 19:28

4 Leviticus 19:27

5 Isaiah 49:16, AMP

6 James 5:12

7 Matthew 23:4, MSG

8 Mark 7:13

9 Mark 7:9

10 1 John 2:15, KJV

11 Matthew 23:23–24, MSG

12 Romans 16:16

13 See Romans 16:16, 1 Corinthians 16:20, 2 Corinthians 13:12, 1 Thessalonians 5:26, 1 Peter 5:14

14 J. I. Packer, *"Fundamentalism" and the Word of God* (Grand Rapids: Eerdmans, 1958) 69–70.

15 1 John 3:3

16 2 Timothy 4:8

17 John 14:1

18 Hebrews 11:16

19 James 2:10–11, author's paraphrase

20 Daniel 4:17

21 Matthew 5:45

22 Psalms 139:17

23 Ephesians 3:18, NLT

24 Acts 17:26

25 Psalm 139:16

26 See Psalm 139:13

27 See 1 Thessalonians 5:21

28 Ecclesiastes 1:9

29 1 Corinthians 15:29

30 Deuteronomy 29:29

31 Ephesians 3:20

32 Romans 15:4

>>chapter 09

1 See Ezekiel 33:11

2 Matthew 25:41

3 2 Peter 3:9, emphasis added

4 John 16:12

5 Jeremiah 33:3

6 See Acts 14:17, James 1:17

7 2 Peter 2:12

8 Isaiah 2:19

9 D. A. Carson, interview with Lee Strobel, quoted in Strobel, *The Case for Christ: A Journalist's Personal Investigation of the Evidence for Jesus* (Grand Rapids: Zondervan, 1998), 164–66.

10 Dermot A. Lane, www.findarticles.com/p/articles/mi_qn4161/is_/ai_N14478904.

11 2 Peter 3:9 MSG

12 Romans 2:14–16, MSG

13 Hebrews 9:27, NLT

14 Joshua 24:15

15 See 1 Thessalonians 5:23

16 www.simonys.oxac.uk/dawkins/worldofdawkins-archive/catalano/quotes/shtml.

17 Charles Templeton, interview with Lee Strobel, quoted in Strobel, *Case for Faith*, 172.

18 John Calvin, *Commentary on a Harmony of the Evangelists, Matthew, Mark, and Luke*, trans. William Pringle (Grand Rapids: Eerdmans, 1949, reprint from 1610), 200–201.

19 William Crockett, *Four Views on Hell* (Grand Rapids: Zondervan 1996), 44.

20 Aristotle, *Nicomachean Ethics*, tran. Martin Ostwald, (Upper Saddle River, NJ: Prentice Hall, 1999), para. 1180a: 29.

21 Romans 2:4–6, MSG

22 Luke 14:26

23 Matthew 5:29

24 See Revelation 21:23–24

25 1 Corinthians 2:9

26 Crockett, *Four Views on Hell*, 47.

27 Jonathan Edwards, in John Gerstner, *Jonathan Edwards on Heaven and Hell* (Grand Rapids: Baker, 1980), 56, n. 37; cf. 54–55.

28 J. P. Moreland, interview with Lee Strobel, quoted in Strobel, *The Case for Faith*, 176.

29 See Revelation 19:12

30 See Revelation 19:15

31 Hebrews 12:29

32 Luke 13:28

33 Moreland interview, Strobel, *Case for Faith,* 177.

34 1 John 4:19

35 McManus, *Chasing Daylight,* 5.

36 Habakkuk 2:14

37 Matthew 5:13–14

38 Mark 11:24

39 *The Book of Common Prayer*, Oxford University Press: New York, 1990, 258.

40 Acts 2:17

41 Psalm 2:8

42 Ephesians 3:20, emphasis added

43 Revelation 21:3–4

44 Matthew 6:10, KJV, emphasis added

45 Hebrews 6:5

46 *Book of Common Prayer,* 138.

>>final thoughts

1 John 6:66–69, MSG

2 1 Corinthians 13:12

3 Mark 9:24

4 Dallas Willard, interview with Lee Strobel, quoted in Strobel, *Case for Faith,* 253.

>>ABOUT THE AUTHOR

Ed Gungor became a follower of Christ as a teenager in the early 1970s and has been deeply involved in the spiritual formation of others for over thirty-five years. Ed has a passion for authentic transformation, a phenomenon he feels is all too rare in today's Church.

As a self-described "church futurist," he is constantly aware of the changing needs of the next generation of Christians. Ed is known for his down-to-earth and engaging communication style. Gungor enthusiastically cuts through the usual "church-speak," gleefully slaughtering any sacred cows that distort the true message of Christ. He is the author of several books, including *There Is More to the* Secret, which landed on the *New York Times* bestsellers list. He has also written *Religiously Transmitted Diseases: Finding a Cure When Faith Doesn't Feel Right* and *The Vow: An Ancient Path of Spiritual Formation That Still Transforms Today.*

Ed and his wife, Gail, have been married thirty years. They have four children and live in Tulsa, Oklahoma. Ed currently serves as lead pastor at Sanctuary in Tulsa and travels around the U.S. and abroad speaking in churches, universities, and seminars. For more information, visit *www.edgungor.com/*.

THE Author, Book & Conversation

Ed Gungor

How writing caught my interest…

Probably the thing that got me thinking seriously about writing was a war movie I saw back in the 80s—I don't remember the title, but in the show the main character decided to focus his life on writing because he believed words could do the most to change how people think. The thought stuck with me and I started working on sharpening my writing skills. It took me almost 20 years to get published, but writing is a dream come true for me.

What I love…

Now in my fifties, I've proven to myself that nothing I accomplish and no position I hold ever really touches my soul—those things are sort of like fingernails. I feel things that touch my nails, but those touches feel sort of "distant" to my body. Attached, yes, but distant. So, the older I get, the more I enjoy working on the things that really touch me: my bride of 30+ years, my kids and grandkids, my friends, and my God—my relationships are what impact my soul. I do love to work, but not at the expense of the people in my life. In theory, I always believed that to be true; I practice it now. Often, old guys are better guys—my wife, Gail, tells me that's happening with me. Thank God.

What was the spark that motivated you to write this book?
We may not like it, but faith is an untidy enterprise. It demands persistence in the face of uncertainty and doubt. Some mistakenly think faith completely eliminates the presence of doubt, and that if doubt is present, it is an indicator that you don't have faith. But I don't think that is true. For many people of faith, the idea of experiencing doubt *at all* makes them nervous. They view the questions that naturally rise in their minds as a lack of faith, which—they fear—surely disqualifies them from being authentic believers. I wrote *What Bothers Me Most about Christianity* because I don't think that is true. I think honest questions and doubt are the fodder of faith—that real faith has doubt and questioning in the mix. That means struggling with doubts and questions is not a lack of faith; it actually *is* faith.

What is the key thought you want readers to take away from this book?
Lots of folks try to make faith a black-and-white issue, but it's not. It is filled with complexity. When it comes to truth in general, most prefer black and white and resist complexity. Complexity is too colorful. We prefer doling out black-and-white conclusions. Telling people *what* seems so much simpler than telling them *why*. And safer too. Indoctrinating people into thinking and acting in certain ways is so clean, so black-and-white simple. Helping them internalize the *why* behind beliefs and actions, and letting them participate in a discussion on conclusions, is both cumbersome and potentially dangerous—they may conclude something different than we do. *God forbid.*

But in a 21st century, pluralistic society, knowing the beliefs and rules of our "in group" will not win the day. We need to know *why* we believe what we believe as opposed to what others say. We need to be "out"-doctrinated—to be shown all sides of an issue, and given the grace and room to draw our own conclusions. In the short haul that may seem crazy and dangerous, but in the end, it is our only option if faith is to survive in the West.

Why did you choose to approach this topic, even though it may be somewhat controversial?
I'm part of a generation that touted, "Jesus is the answer." In a sense, we thought faith answered all the questions of our time and believed a questioning mind revealed you had not yet experienced faith. The apostle Paul penned, "Now to him who is able to do immeasurably more than all we ask. . ." (Eph. 3:20). God can afford any question

we can come up with. But many try to avoid the natural questions that come into the modern mind over matters of faith. We work to systematize everything: our beliefs, our experiences, our outcomes—we want to have a clear understanding about everything we say and believe. We no more appreciate mystery and questions than we do appendicitis.

But there are many things we believe that rest in the domain of mystery. I'm not saying we shouldn't try to figure them out, but after we try and still come up empty, we need to smile and be OK with questions. The Greek Orthodox Church speaks of *apophatic* theology, a theology that celebrates what we *don't* know about faith and about God. Paul said it this way: "Oh, the depth of the riches of the wisdom and knowledge of God! How unsearchable his judgments, and his paths beyond tracing out!" (Rom. 11:33).

I'm no longer sure we had it right when we told people "Jesus is the answer." What if he's the question? What if the million-dollar question is *What are you going to do with Jesus and his claims?* And what if faith is really about all the questions that emerge from that conversation?

***Shouldn't we be guarded about truth (*orthodoxy)?**

Most of us appreciate the familiar. We feel safer. We generally believe the things told to us by the people we trust. Other opinions about truth-positions often feel dangerous because they call into question not only our beliefs on a particular subject, but also the in-group we are part of. However, it is instructive to listen to different views of Christ followers (both living and from history). Many issues of faith are not as clear as they first seem, and listening to each other broadens us in healthy ways.

It is definitely appropriate to *disagree* with other Christians after we hear the defense for their positions; it is just not appropriate to be *disagreeable*. We should have great difficulty with absolutism and accusatory language in our discussions, along with any willingness to dismiss the views of others as "compromise" or "of Satan." That kind of positioning is counterproductive, not prophetic. Planting flags and spouting overly simplistic tautologies cause us to fall short of doing anything transformational. It simply draws lines in the sand—not unlike political debates that are not about finding solutions and synergies, but simply serve to establish "us/them" identification markers. Always bad form.

How can we change the world?

It is evident that the church is walking into a dark night of deep cultural displacement. Our old hegemonies—the ways we influenced the world—are passing away. The old symbols of safety—big church buildings, political power, a *Leave It to Beaver* culture, and so on—are becoming more and more a thing of the past. What is needed in these coming days is a prophetic people, tethered to the vision of the kingdom of God through lively confession and prophetic praxis. By so living, we do a couple of things: 1) we show that the kingdoms of our world are less than they think they are; and 2) we embody our salvation in real time in real circumstances—we offer "salvation" to the kingdoms of the world. We need to be, as Paul puts it in Philippians, a *politeuma*— a robust, lively "colony of heaven" situated right smack in the middle of the chaos of pagan culture.

Remember, it was Jesus who cried, "I will build my church, and the gates of Hades will not overcome it." Notice *who* is supposed to be "gated" in Jesus' view. The church is not supposed to be inside a gated fortress . . . "holding on" till Jesus comes. We're supposed to be attacking the dark forces. God doesn't abandon cultures. He doesn't want us enclaved into gated Christian communities waiting for the return of his Son. He wants us to bring his salvation to the ends of the earth as his faithful few.

This means we are going to need to be able to deal with the honest questions that those outside of faith frequently ask. Questions about reason, church history, the why of evil, etc.—these are vital questions for us to become familiar with in order to be a voice for God in this era.

1. Does it bother you that God is intentionally hiding? Why or why not?

2. Does it bother you that reason doesn't always lead one to faith?

3. Does it bother you that God allows evil in the world? What do you personally believe about evil? What role does Satan, people, or God play in it?

4. Does it bother you that Jesus is the only way to a relationship with God? What about those who have never heard or understood the message about Jesus?

5. Does it bother you that some see science and faith as incompatible? Where do you think they intersect or collide? What do you do when science and faith seem to contradict each other?

6. Does it bother you that so many Christians give Christianity a bad name? What do you do when people bring up the negative reputation of Christians?

7. Does it bother you that God looks like such a bully in the Old Testament? What are your thoughts about the matter?

8. Does it bother you that believers constantly misuse sacred text? How do you approach Scripture in your study life?

9. Does it bother you that the Christian faith includes a hell? Are you convinced in the literal or metaphorical view of the descriptions of hell?

10. Do questions about faith bother you? Why or why not?